# At the Feet of My Master

Cyprus Summer Series, Volume 2

# At the Feet of My Master

## Sufi Guidance for the 21st Century

By

Shaykh Muhammad Hisham Kabbani

Institute for Spiritual and Cultural Advancement

Published and Distributed by:

Institute for Spiritual and Cultural Advancement (ISCA)
17195 Silver Parkway, #401
Fenton, MI 48430 USA
Tel: (888) 278-6624
Fax: (810) 815-0518
Email: staff@naqshbandi.org
Web: http://www.naqshbandi.org

First Edition: May 2010
CYPRUS SUMMER SERIES, Volume 2

Library of Congress Control Number: 2009936511

Kabbani, Muhammad Hisham.

At the Feet of My Master: spiritual wisdom for the 21st Century / Muhammad Hisham Kabbani. -- 1st ed.

P. cm.

Includes bibliographical references.

ISBN 978-1-930409-73-6 (alk. paper)

1. Naqshabandiyah. 2. Sufism. 3. Sufis--Biography. I. Title.

BP189.7.N352K33 2009

297.4"8--dc22

2009936511

PRINTED IN THE UNITED STATES OF AMERICA

15 14 13 12 11 05 06 07 08 09

The author sitting at the feet of his master, Sultan al-Awliya of this century, Mawlana Shaykh Muhammad Nazim Adil al-Haqqani, head of the Most Distinguished Naqshbandi-Haqqani Sufi Order at the global center in Lefke, Cyprus. 2009.

# Contents

ABOUT THE AUTHOR ..... I
PREFACE ..... III
PUBLISHER'S NOTES ..... V
RECITATION BEFORE EVERY ASSOCIATION ..... IX
NAQSHBANDI-HAQQANI GOLDEN CHAIN ..... XI
FOREWORD ..... XIII
MURSHID AT-TABARRUK: GUIDE OF BLESSINGS ..... 1
Definition of a Guide in Tariqah ..... 1
Basic Characteristics of Murshid at-Tabarruk ..... 3
Grandshaykh's Request to Raise His Followers ..... 10
Knowing the Benefits and Names of All Creation ..... 12
Heavenly Attendants at the Throne of Allah ..... 16
The Direct Connection and Awrad ..... 17
Make Rabitah to the Shaykh ..... 19
Seventeen Signs on His Face ..... 22
The Traps of Arrogance ..... 23
MURSHID AT-TAZKIYYAH: GUIDE OF PURIFICATION ..... 29
Consequences of Backbiting and Breaking Hearts ..... 34
Confusion in Our Ranks ..... 37
Laziness Blocks Higher Levels of Knowledge ..... 40
Sultan Salim and Muhiyuddin Ibn al-Arabi ..... 43
Be Purified through Your Sadaqa ..... 48
The Murshid Observes and Tests His Followers ..... 51
Murshid at-Tazkiyyah Purifies His Followers ..... 57
Surrender Like Sayyidina Ibrahim ..... 58
Sultan adh-Dhikr ..... 67
MURSHID AT-TASFIYYAH: GUIDE OF SIFTING ..... 75
Characteristics of Murshid at-Tasfiyyah ..... 76
More Characteristics of Murshid at-Tasfiyyah ..... 84
Obligations and Forbiddens ..... 87
The Disciple and the Rat ..... 92
Five Levels of the Heart ..... 94
Seeing the Signs of Allah's Oneness ..... 98
MURSHID AT-TARBIYYAH: GUIDE OF EDUCATION ..... 105
Humility of Murshid at-Tarbiyyah ..... 105
The Station and Powers of Murshid at-Tarbiyyah ..... 113
Story of Shaykh Ahmad al-Badawi ..... 118
Guardian of Your Divine Trust ..... 124
The Wisdom of Saints and Idiocy of Their Followers ..... 131
Ways of Moral Excellence ..... 140
How the Secret Was Passed to Mawlana Shaykh ..... 148
ISLAMIC CALENDAR AND HOLY DAYS ..... 159
GLOSSARY ..... 163
OTHER PUBLICATIONS OF INTEREST ..... 171

# About the Author

As a world-renowned religious scholar, Shaykh Muhammad Hisham Kabbani is featured in the book, *The 500 Most Influential Muslims* published in November 2009. Throughout his life he has promoted traditional Islamic principles of peace, tolerance, love, compassion and brotherhood, while rigorously opposing extremism in all its forms. He hails from a respected family of traditional Islamic scholars, which includes the former head of the Association of Muslim Scholars of Lebanon and the present grand mufti (highest Islamic religious authority) of Lebanon.

Shaykh Kabbani is highly trained, both as a Western scientist and an Islamic scholar. He received a bachelor's degree in chemistry and later studied medicine. Under the instruction of Shaykh ʿAbdAllāh ad-Dāghestānī, upon whose personal notes this book is based, he holds a degree in Islamic Divine Law. Shaykh Muhammad Nazim Adil al-Haqqani, world leader of the Naqshbandi-Haqqani Sufi Order, authorized him to teach and counsel students in Sufism.

In his long-standing endeavor to promote a better understanding of traditional Islam, in February 2010, Shaykh Kabbani hosted HRH Charles, the Prince of Wales at a cultural event at the revered Old Trafford stadium in Manchester, U.K. He has hosted two international conferences in the U.S., and regional conferences on a host of issues, which attracted moderate Muslim scholars from Asia, the Far East, Middle East, Africa, U.K. and Eastern Europe. His counsel is sought by journalists, academics, and government leaders.

For more than three decades, Shaykh Kabbani has consistently promoted peaceful cooperation among people of all beliefs. Since the early 1990s, he has launched numerous endeavors to bring moderate Muslims into the mainstream.

Often at great personal risk, he has been instrumental in awakening Muslim social consciousness regarding the religious duty to stand firm against extremism and terrorism, for the benefit of the world and its future generations. His bright, hopeful outlook, with a goal to honor and serve all humanity, has helped millions understand the difference between moderate, mainstream Muslims and minority extremist sects.

In the United States, Shaykh Kabbani serves as Chairman, Islamic Supreme Council of America; Founder, Naqshbandi Sufi Order of America; Advisor, World Organization for Resource Development and Education; Chairman, As-Sunnah Foundation of America; Chairman, Kamilat Muslim Women's Organization; and Founder, *The Muslim Magazine*. In the United Kingdom, Shaykh Kabbani is an advisor to Sufi Muslim Council, which consults to the British government on public policy and timely social and religious issues.

Other titles by Shaykh Kabbani include: *The Nine-fold Ascent* (2009), *At the Feet of My Master, Volume 1* (2009), *Banquet for the Soul* (2008), *Illuminations* (2007), *Universe Rising* (2007), *Symphony of Remembrance* (2007), *A Spiritual Commentary on the Chapter of Sincerity* (2006), *Sufi Science of Self-Realization* (Fons Vitae, 2005), *Keys To the Divine Kingdom* (2005), *Classical Islam and the Naqshbandi Sufi Order* (2004), *The Naqshbandi Sufi Tradition Guidebook* (2004), *The Approach of Armageddon? An Islamic Perspective* (2003), *Encyclopaedia of Muhammad's Women Companions and the Traditions They Related* (1998, with Dr. Laleh Bakhtiar), *Encyclopaedia of Islamic Doctrine* (7 vols. 1998), *Angels Unveiled* (1996), *The Naqshbandi Sufi Way* (1995), *and Remembrance of God Liturgy of the Sufi Naqshbandi Masters* (1994).

# *Preface*

The rare hundred-year-old manuscript upon which this book is based is taken from personal notes of Sayyīdinā Shaykh Sharafuddīn ad-Daghestani (d. 1936), the 38th shaykh of the esteemed Naqshbandi-Haqqani Golden Chain. It consists of more than 4000 pages.

In summer 2008 at his center in Lefke, Cyprus, for the first time my spiritual master, Mawlana Shaykh Nazim Adil al-Haqqani, instructed me to present *ṣuḥbahs* (extemporaneous, spiritually inspired talks) to seekers from all over the world. Thus, the "Cyprus Summer Series" was born, to which we hope to add future material. This is Volume Two of the series.

Explanations herein are particularly directed to those who understand the Sufi Way, who have previously accompanied saints, and who are willing to open their minds and hearts to the intense love of Allāh, His messenger, and the spiritual guides.

For seekers of the guidance to overcome destructive character traits, or to develop one's personal connection to the Creator, it is hoped this book will touch your heart in ways that promote lasting, unprecedented spiritual growth.

*Shaykh Muhammad Hisham Kabbani,*
*Representative of Mawlana Shaykh Nazim Adil al-Haqqani,*
*40th Shaykh in the Naqshbandi-Haqqani Golden Chain*

# Publisher's Notes

This book is directed to those familiar with the Sufi Way; however, to accommodate lay readers unfamiliar with Sufi terminology and practices, we have provided English translations of Arabic texts and a comprehensive glossary. Where Arabic terms are crucial to the discussion, we have included transliteration and footnoted explanations. For readers familiar with Arabic and Islamic teachings, for further clarity please consult the cited sources.

The original material is based on transcripts of a series of holy gatherings which serve as conduits of heavenly guidance. The *ṣuḥbah,* a divinely inspired talk which conveys powerful energy that uplifts the soul, is delivered by the "shaykh," a highly trained spiritual guide. To present the authentic flavor of such rare teachings, great care was taken to preserve the speaking styles of both the author and the illustrious shaykhs upon whose notes this book is based.

Translations from Arabic to English pose unique challenges which we have tried our best to make understandable to Western readers. In addition, please note the worldwide cultural practice to not include the definite article "the," as in "~~the~~ Prophet," which is a more intimate reference that appears occasionally throughout this work.

Quotes from the Holy Qur'an are offset, with chapter number and verse cited. The Holy Traditions of Prophet Muhammad *(āḥadīth)* are offset and cited, in most cases. Historic dates are often referenced as "Hijri" and "A.H." (After Hijri), which is the commencement of the Islamic calendar, when Prophet Muhammad migrated from Mecca to Madinah in 622 C.E. (Christian Era) to escape religious persecution and form his early nation. A reference calendar has also been provided.

Where gender-specific pronouns such as "he" and "him" are applied in a general sense, no discrimination is intended towards women, upon whom The Almighty bestowed great honor.

Islamic teachings are primarily based on four sources, in this order:

- **Holy Qur'an**: the holy book of divine revelation (God's Word) granted to Prophet Muhammad. Reference to Holy Qur'an appears as "4:12," indicating "Chapter 4, Verse 12."
- **Sunnah**: holy traditions of Prophet Muhammad ﷺ; the systematic recording of his words and actions that comprise the *ḥadīth*. For fifteen centuries, Islam has applied a strict, highly technical standard, rating each narration in terms of its authenticity and categorizing its "transmission." As this book is not highly technical, we simplified the reporting of *ḥadīth*, but included the narrator and source texts to support the discussion at hand.
- ***Ijma'***: The adherence, or agreement of the experts of independent reasoning *(āhl al-ijtihād)* to the conclusions of a given ruling pertaining to what is permitted and what is forbidden after the passing of the Prophet, Peace be upon him, as well as the agreement of the Community of Muslims concerning what is obligatorily known of the religion with its decisive proofs. Perhaps a clearer statement of this principle is, "We do not separate (in belief and practice) from the largest group of the Muslims."
- **Legal Rulings:** highly trained Islamic scholars form legal rulings from their interpretation of the Qur'an and the Sunnah, known as *ijtihād.* Such rulings are intended to provide Muslims an Islamic context regarding contemporary social norms. In theological terms, scholars who form legal opinions have completed many years of rigorous training and possess degrees similar to a doctorate in divinity in Islamic knowledge, or in legal

terms, hold the status of a high court or supreme court judge, or higher.

The following universally recognized symbols have been respectfully included in this work. While they may seem tedious, they are deeply appreciated by a vast majority of our readers.

سبحانه وتعالى *subḥānahu wa ta'ala* (may His Glory be Exalted), recited after the name "Allāh" and any of the Islamic names of God.

ﷺ *ṣallAllāhu 'alayhi wa sallam* (God's blessings and greetings of peace be upon him), recited after the holy name of Prophet Muhammad.

عليه السلام *'alayhi 's-salām* (peace be upon him/her), recited after holy names of other prophets, names of Prophet Muhammad's relatives, the pure and virtuous women in Islam, and angels.

رضي الله عنه / رضي الله عنهم *raḍīAllāhu 'anh(um)* (may God be pleased with him/her), recited after the holy names of Companions of Prophet Muhammad; plural: *raḍīAllāhu 'anhum.*

ق represents *qaddasAllāhu sirrah* (may God sanctify his secret), recited after names of saints.

## Transliteration

Transliteration from Arabic to English poses challenges. To show respect, Muslims often capitalize nouns which, in English, normally appear in lowercase. To facilitate authentic pronunciation of names, places and terms, use the following key:

| Symbol | Transliteration | Symbol | Transliteration | Vowels: Long | |
|---|---|---|---|---|---|
| ء | ‘ | ط | ṭ | آ ى | ā |
| ب | b | ظ | ẓ | و | ū |
| ت | t | ع | ʿ | ي | ī |
| ث | th | غ | gh | **Short** | |
| ج | j | ف | f | َ | a |
| ح | ħ | ق | q | ُ | u |
| خ | kh | ك | k | ِ | i |
| د | d | ل | l | | |
| ذ | dh | م | m | | |
| ر | r | ن | n | | |
| ز | z | ه | h | | |
| س | s | و | w | | |
| ش | sh | ي | y | | |
| ص | š | ة | ah; at | | |
| ض | ḍ | ال | al-/'l- | | |

# Recitation before Every Association

بسم الله الرحمن الرحيم

*A'ūdhu billāhi min ash-Shayṭān ir-rajīm.*
*Bismil-Lāhi' r-Raḥmāni 'r-Raḥīm.*
*Nawaytu 'l-arbā'īn, nawaytu 'l-'itikāf,*
*nawaytu'l-khalwah, nawaytu 'l-'uzlah,*
*nawaytu 'r-riyāḍa, nawaytu 's-sulūk,*
*lillāhi ta'ala fī hādhā 'l-masjid, al-maqām*
*Sayyiduna Shaykh Muḥammad Nāẓim al-Ḥaqqānī.*

*Ati' ūllah wa ati' ūr-Rasūl*
*wa ūli'l-amri minkūm.*

*I seek refuge in Allāh from Satan, the rejected.*
*In the name of Allāh, the Merciful,*
*the Compassionate.*
*I intend the forty (days of seclusion);*
*I intend seclusion in the mosque,*
*I intend seclusion, I intend isolation,*
*I intend discipline (of the ego); I intend to travel*
*in God's Path for the sake of God,*
*in this mosque, in the maqām of our Master,*
*Mawlana Shaykh Nazim al-Haqqani.*

*Obey Allāh, obey the Prophet,*
*and obey those in authority among you.*
*Sūratu 'n-Nisā (The Women), 4:59*

# Naqshbandi-Haqqani Golden Chain

*May Allāh ﷻ preserve their secrets.*

**Prophet** Muḥammad **ibn ʿAbdAllāh** ﷺ
Abū Bakr as-Ṣiddīq
Salmān al-Farsi
Qasim bin Muḥammad bin AbūBakr
Jafar as-Ṣādiq
Tayfur Abū Yazid al-Bistāmi
Abūl Hassan ʿAlī al-Kharqani
Abū ʿAlī al-Farmadi
Abū Yaqub Yusuf al-Hamadani
Abūl Abbas, al-Khiḍr
Abdul Khaliq al-Ghujdawani
Arif ar-Riwakri
Khwaja Mahmoud al-Anjir al-Faghnawi
ʿAlī ar-Ramitani
Muḥammad Baba as-Samasi
As-Sayyid Amir Kulal
Muḥammad Bahauddin Shah Naqshband
Alauddīn al-Bukhārī al-Attar
Yaqub al-Charkhi
Ubaydullāh al-Ahrar
Muḥammad az-Zāhid
Darwish Muḥammad
Muḥammad Khwaja al-Amkanaki
Muḥammad al-Baqi bilLah
Aḥmad al-Farūqi as-Sirhindi
Muḥammad al-Masum
Muḥammad Sayfuddin al-Farūqi al-Mujaddidi
As-Sayyid Nūr Muḥammad al-Badawani
Shamsuddin Habīb Allāh
ʿAbdAllāh ad-Dahlawi
Khalid al-Baghdadi
Ismail Muḥammad ash-Shirwani
Khas Muḥammad Shirwani
Muḥammad Effendi al-Yaraghi
Jamaluddin al-Ghumuqi al-Husayni
Abū Aḥmad as-Sughuri
Abū Muḥammad al-Madani
Sharafuddīn ad-Dāghestānī
ʿAbdAllāh al-Fāʾiz ad-Dāghestānī
Muḥammad Nāẓim al-Ḥaqqānī

# *Foreword*

This timely collection of *ṣuḥbahs* (inspired spiritual discourses) is based on teachings of Sufi masters of the illustrious Naqshbandi Golden Chain, taken directly from notes of the current Sufi master, Shaykh Muhammad Nazim Adil al-Haqqani.

This second volume of the *Cyprus Summer Series* is comprised of eighteen *ṣuḥbahs* by Shaykh Hisham Kabbani at the direction of his master, Mawlana Shaykh Nazim. They represent but a drop of the divine wisdoms poured from the heart of the master into the heart of the student.

You are now presented with this gift, *At the Feet of My Master, Volume 2,* a treasure which should be guarded.

The contents of this book are intended to clarify important issues of *ṭarīqah* (the Sufi Way), so readers can better understand the mission of the Naqshbandi Sufi Order and the high position of the Sufi masters, the *awlīyā* (saints), and our beloved Prophet Muhammad ﷺ.

We hope this series will help readers increase their love for the present Sulṭān al-Awlīyā, Mawlana Shaykh Nazim, and for the Seal of Prophets, Sayyīdīna Muhammad ﷺ, and Allāh Almighty, to receive the endless blessings, favors and divine love Allāh ﷻ is ever ready to pour into the hearts of His Creation in every moment. It is also dearly hoped readers will be able to practice the teachings of our master with more sincerity and make quick progress on the spiritual path.

By the hand of our master, Mawlana Shaykh Nazim, we are asking Allāh Almighty to grant that we reach the spiritual presence of the forty masters of the Naqshbandi Golden Chain, to Prophet Muhammad ﷺ, and finally, to the Unity Oceans of

Allāh Almighty, the spiritual homeland of our souls, to where He calls us and patiently awaits our arrival.

We are asking Allāh Almighty to hasten the appearances of Sayyidina Imām Mahdī ﷺ and Sayyidinā ʿĪsā ﷺ, and grant us to be with them, together with our Master, the Inheritor of Prophet Muhammad ﷺ, Mawlana Shaykh Muhammad Nazim Adil al-Haqqani, may Allāh grant him health, a long life, and the fulfillment of the noble promise he made on the Day of Promises. *Amīn.*

May Allāh bless Prophet Muhammad ﷺ, his noble Family and beloved Companions ﷺ. Praise and thanks be to the Lord of the Worlds.

1

# Murshid at-Tabarruk: Guide of Blessings

*Madad yā Sulṭān al-Awlīyā, Shaykh Muḥammad Nāẓim al-Ḥaqqānī.*
*Madad yā Sulṭān al-Awlīyā, Shaykh ʿAbdAllāh al-Fā'iz ad-Dāghestānī.*

From Mawlana Shaykh Nazim's and Grandshaykh ʿAbdAllāh ad-Daghestani's notes from a long time ago, we hope to learn what are the characteristics of guides, and who is —and who is not—a guide. This is a very important series of *ṣuḥbahs* that will help clarify what is a guide, *inshāAllāh,* as these days too many people are declaring they are guides and it creates confusion and brings hardship on people.

## Definition of a Guide in Tariqah

Sulṭān al-Awlīyā, Mawlana Shaykh Muhammad Nazim al-Haqqani, may Allāh give him long life, now gives everyone authorization to lead *dhikrullāh* because he wants to spread knowledge of the Naqshbandi Ṭarīqah. If they have been given permission or authorization to lead *dhikrullāh* and make a circle for the remembrance of Allāh's ﷻ Beautiful Names and Attributes to call people from every walk of life, some begin to believe attendees are *their* followers and *they* are the shaykh or guide for that group.

Yesterday Mawlana Shaykh told a guest, "I like for you to do group *dhikr* in your home."

That one answered, "I am attending *dhikr* with this authorized one."

Mawlana explained, "Okay, lead *dhikr* in your home because more people will come as they might be far from that other person and with the *barakah* of *dhikr,* you can continue once a month to meet all together."

Now from that, some people might misunderstand they are already authorized and they begin to act as if they are a guide. You find many websites today all over the world hosted by people claiming they are the authorized guide for this and that.

First of all, a guide has to be for the whole *Ummah,* not for 10, 50 or 100 people. In *ṭarīqah,* the guide is *al-Murshid* who has reached Maqām al-Irshād, the Level of Guidance. Our understanding of the term "guidance" is more comprehensive than what many understand. In *ṭarīqah,* guidance is not just to give you a presentation like a professor in a university or a scholar in a *masjid,* to whom you may listen and if you like it or not, he doesn't care. But a genuine guide in *ṭarīqah* is responsible to care for you and guide you from one spiritual level to another until you reach the holy presence of Prophet ﷺ.

I hope to shed light on this important topic, because many people think they are the guide of this or that country, or this or that street, or that alley, or that house, or that village, or even that shack or barn, or that farm! It is a big issue and a problem. I hope that from this place, Mawlana Shaykh Nazim's house and *masjid,* from their holy notes we find a definition of the characteristics of a guide.

There are different kinds of guides, and the most important is what Grandshaykh ق, described:

1. **Murshid at-Tabarruk:** the Guide of Blessing.

2. **Murshid at-Tazkīyyah:** the Guide of Purification

3. **Murshid at-Taṣfīyyah:** the Guide who sifts *murīds* from the other two guides and takes the purest.

4. **Murshid at-Tarbīyyah:** (or Murshid al-Wilāyah); the highest of the four; the Guide who carries all the others and raises them up through spiritual levels. He is Sulṭān al-Awlīyā.

We must not be confused by anyone who says, "I am *khalīfah*/ deputy/ representative of Mawlana Shaykh." I am addressing Mawlana Shaykh's followers around the world, and many are making that claim. From the first line of Grandshaykh notes that I am quoting here, you can realize not one of those *murīds* is a *murshid*, not on their websites, not in different countries, not in any capacity whatsoever! They may lead *dhikr* or teach from Mawlana Shaykh's teachings, but they are not a *khalīfah* or guide.

## Basic Characteristics of Murshid at-Tabarruk

From Grandshaykh's teachings, we find Mawlana Shaykh's first explanation of Murshid at-Tabarruk, from whom you take *barakah*. Even if you don't do anything—no *tasbīḥ*, no *dhikr*, no *ṣadaqah*—he is like a spotlight and his presence will attract you. All the characteristics of Murshid at-Tabarruk must be also with the next level of guide, Murshid at-Tazkīyyah. The second level of *murshid* must have the first level of *murshid's* characteristics; the third level of *murshid* must have the second level *murshid's* characteristics, and the fourth level of *murshid* must have all characteristics of the previous three levels.

Murshid at-Tabarruk is the first level of *irshād*, and some of his characteristics are:

- He has been authorized by his shaykh, Murshid at-Tabarruk, before he addresses or guides anyone.
- He must guide his *murīds* through a dark tunnel that has a beginning but no end.
- He must try to take his *murīds* all the way to their destiny, and like a shepherd guarding his sheep, he must guard his *murīds* from dangers of wild animals all around.
- He has to receive authorization (*ijāzah*) from his shaykh, along with the power that enables him to inherit directly

from the tongue of Prophet ﷺ and give that knowledge to those in his circle, and put on their tongue *at-talqīn.*[1]

- When Murshid at-Tabarruk recites *"Allāh, Allāh,"* at that moment he receives or is dressed in Allāh's ninety-nine Beautiful Names and Attributes and their divine secrets.
- He must know every language of all Creation.

When Allāh ﷻ told Sayyīdīnā Muhammad ﷺ, *Qul Hūw Allāhu Āḥad, "Say: He is Allāh, the Unique,"* Allāh put that reality on Prophet's ﷺ tongue and in his heart. For this reason, the shaykh has to put that guidance on the tongue of the one who needs to receive it, his *murīd*.

Prophet ﷺ said, "If anyone wants to see a dead person before he died, look at Abū Bakr aṣ-Ṣiddīq." It means to achieve that level of guidance you have to possess that characteristic. Murshid at-Tabarruk cannot reach the level of *irshād* until his ego dies in this life, and then he will inherit from his shaykh, and Prophet ﷺ will put on his tongue Tawqīn adh-Dhikr (how to recite *dhikrullāh* 5,000 times daily). In Naqshbandi Ṭarīqah, when you take *baya*ʿ you must establish the daily *wird* (practices) of reciting 5,000 times daily *Allāh, Allāh* through the heart and on the tongue. Today we are imitating the real practice, but when one reaches the level of Murshid at-Tabarruk, "by tongue and by heart" means you put your tongue on the ceiling of your mouth when you recite *Allāh, Allāh* and see your heart is also reciting *Allāh, Allāh* in unison with your tongue.

---

[1] A *sunnah* of Prophet ﷺ to recite *shahādah* at time of death, and is well established in Shari`ah. A worldwide Islamic tradition is to say at the graveside or over the newly deceased, *Qul, Yā `AbdAllāh!* "O Servant of Allāh, remember to recite (*shahādah*)!"

*Irshād* has rules that they gave us in writing, but there are rules from heart to heart that you cannot explain and there is no permission to discuss them. I am speaking to those who are watching from around the world on Sufilive.com; these are important characteristics of *murshids*. Today many people are confused about this issue and that is a contagious sickness like Swine Flu, spreading from the unauthorized one who believes himself to be a *murshid* to all his followers. When you cheat your people, those who believe in you, you become more filthy than a pig. You have to be very careful. I'm saying this out of love, because we don't want people to fall into the trap of Shayṭān. Not everyone can truthfully declare, "I am *khalīfah*," or "I am a *murshid*."

In Naqshbandi Ṭarīqah, when you recite "Allāh, Allāh," you did your *waẓīfah*, your job, your duty. Beyond that, every time you recite *Allāh, Allāh* you receive spiritual emanations from that authorized *murshid*, who dresses you in a manifestation of Allāh's Beautiful Names and Attributes! If you cannot comprehend it at least you will feel the beauty of it.

So I ask now, who can have that? Those who are calling themselves *murshid* today, do they possess these characteristics, or not? It is beyond them.

Grandshaykh ق continues, "Murshid at-Tabarruk has to recite *dhikrullāh* 5,000 times daily in that way I described, and he takes knowledge from it. He must then recite 500 times daily *ṣalawāt* on Prophet ﷺ, *Allāhuma ṣalli ʿalā Muḥammadin wa ʿalā āli Muḥammadin wa sallim.* The lowest level of *barakah* he receives is to experience the beautiful fragrance of Prophet ﷺ; otherwise, he can sense Prophet's holy presence or visualize him through his heart."

Today, what we are doing? We recite *tasbīḥ* while watching TV, or some *murīds* try to impress others by carrying a very long *tasbīḥ*. Until recently, I never saw Mawlana Shaykh

Nazim with a *tasbīḥ* that contained more than 100 beads. Today they carry a thousand beads around their necks; they wrap it on their shoulders and bellies! Mawlana Shaykh had a *tasbīḥ* with a thousand beads for *tahajjud*[2] in his room; when he completes his prayer and is waiting for Fajr, he recites on that *tasbīḥ* of 100 beads, or sometimes 500 beads, but during the day he never carries a *tasbīḥ* of more than 100 beads. I'm not saying don't carry a *tasbīḥ* with 200 beads, but just a reminder that Mawlana Shaykh doesn't show-off or let his ego play with him. When you carry a very long *tasbīḥ* in public, it means, "Look at me because I am so pious!"

That one who is sitting on his couch, proclaiming himself a *murshid* can have rings on all his fingers and a huge turban, and he never knows anything from Sharīʿah! Ask him a question about Islamic Law and he doesn't know how to answer. They don't even lead prayers because they don't know proper recitation of Holy Qur'an or the *adab* of *ṣalāt*, and they make themselves big shaykhs! Unfortunately, these troublemakers are now all around the world.

When Murshid at-Tabarruk recites 500 times *ṣalawāt ʿalā 'n-Nabī* ﷺ, his heart is with his shaykh, Murshid at-Tarbīyyah, the highest one who raises all others, who is directly connected to Prophet ﷺ. So when his *murīd*, Murshid at-Tabarruk says,

---

[2] Ṣalāt at-Tahajjud is the voluntary pre-dawn prayer recommended in Holy Qur'an and hadith for spiritual advancement:
*And during a part of the night, pray Tahajjud beyond what is incumbent on you that perhaps your Lord will raise you to a position of great glory. Sūratu 'l-'Isrā' (17:79).*
*Abū Hurayrah* ؓ *narrated that Prophet Muhammad* ﷺ *said, "Our Lord descends to the lowest heaven during the last third of the night, inquiring, 'Who will call on Me so that I may respond to him? Who is asking something of Me so I may give it to him? Who is asking for My forgiveness so I may forgive him?'" (al-Bukhārī)*

*Allāhuma ṣalli ʿalā Muḥammadin wa ʿalā āli Muḥammadin wa sallim,* his shaykh, Murshid at-Tarbīyyah, will take him all the way to the holy presence of Prophet ﷺ!

This is from only half of the first line of Grandshaykh's and Mawlana Shaykh's explanation of the first level of *murshid*! Does anyone have that? How do these common people claim they are a *murshid*? So this will help us reconsider who is—and who is not—a *murshid.*

I am not saying something to harm anyone; we are defining. Everyone who has authority and permission from Mawlana Shaykh to lead *dhikr* has to understand that Mawlana Shaykh is the *murshid,* not himself. For sure, some people will not accept this teaching or this definition, but those who are interested must reconsider their status. Ask yourself, "What is my level of knowledge? Am I improving? Am I cheating myself and others? Do I truly possess the characteristics Grandshaykh described?

Grandshaykh continues, "Murshid at-Tabarruk must have the capacity and capability of knowing all languages of all Creation, those who have voices and those who do not." Human beings and animals have a voice, and other creatures such as butterflies, worms, leaves and trees you don't hear.

> *And there is not a thing but glorifies His Praise but you understand not their praise.*
>
> *Sūratu 'l-'Isrā' (The Night Journey), 17:44*

A *sunnah* of Prophet ﷺ is to wear a ring on the right hand, to have praises of Allāh ﷻ all the time on your finger. Prophet ﷺ said the best is to wear a ring of *aqīq* (red carnelian) because it has highly special praises, and the second best is a ring of *fayrūz,* turquoise. Murshids wear rings of either stone because they like to hear the rings' praises. With that *ḥikmah* we follow the *sunnah* of Prophet ﷺ, and now for first time Mawlana

Shaykh mentioned the value of the ring, particularly when the stone touches your skin and it gives you very positive energy.

Grandshaykh ق continues, "Murshid at-Tabarruk has to know all different praises, all different languages of everyone Allāh created, human and non-human, and he must have mastered the complete knowledge of every letter of their language and how they speak it (*tafsīr al-ḥurūf*). He must know this power is from his shaykh, who is taking from Prophet ﷺ. Not one voice will separate him from the other voice (he hears all the voices simultaneously, as if with different headsets) and he can differentiate one from another."

Oh brothers and sisters, we must be very careful about proclaiming who is a *murshid*. If you have made this mistake, please reconsider your situation, because if you are not authorized and do not possess these characteristics we have just described, your sickness will reflect on your followers. On the Day of Judgment, Allāh will ask you about why you cheated your followers and made false claims.

May Allāh ﷻ forgive us. We don't declare we are anything; we are the weakest and we have nothing. I have only my shaykh, that is my source. I'm not saying I have anything; I'm lower than the lowest. It's out of love that Mawlana Shaykh made me say this. Be careful! Don't think you have a high status or you will lose.

Today many pretend they are seeing spiritual visions, and mostly they hallucinate or they are imagining. When someone doesn't speak too much and all night he is up, at any moment he doesn't know more than what he speaks, and he might say something from the east or from the west. Also, some people suffer from various psychological disabilities and take medication which causes them to hallucinate. In Grandshaykh's notes he explains that for a *murshid* there is no

doing what I am asking from them. It will be a burden on me and on them."

Shaykh Sharafuddīn ق said, "Then what do you want?"

Grandshaykh ق answered, "Then *yā Sayyīdī*, if you give me something that I like through that *irshād*, then I will accept."

Shaykh Sharafuddīn ق said, "What do you want?"

Grandshaykh ق answered, "Whenever I give a *ṣuḥbah* or advice, I want anyone sitting in my company and listening to me to be raised to the same level I am in at that moment, without them doing anything. I am not even expecting from them to do their *awrād*; if they do it *alḥamdūlillāh*, and if they don't do it, I still want them to be in my level. If I speak about any *walī* in my presentation or in giving advice, I want them to be in the level of that *walī*. If you give me that *irshād* with these specifications then it has a meaning, then at least I will say that these *murīds* have been raised and I will feel happy, or what is the benefit? I will be somewhere and they will be somewhere very far from me. No, if they will be with me because they are in *dunyā* with me, I want also them in *Ākhirah* with me. If I get that, I will accept."

According to Grandshaykh's notes, that night Shaykh Sharafuddīn presented that noble request to Prophet ﷺ through a vision, and Prophet ﷺ said, "*Anā rāḍin, ana rāḍin, ana rāḍin*! I am satisfied, I am satisfied, I am satisfied and I accept!"

So from that kind of *irshād*, Grandshaykh ق said he didn't want it if it's not going to raise the level of *murīds*. So we have to be very careful where we are connecting ourselves. Many people today are misled; they are misled as to their source, of who is their father. Allāh said in Holy Qur'an:

> *Call them to their parents (father). If you don't know their father, say to them, 'You are my brothers.'" Surātu 'l-Aḥzāb,33:5*

Call everyone to their fathers; everyone must know that his spiritual father is his shaykh. It means you cannot call them to the shaykh's representatives. Today people say, "We are followers of this representative or that representative." No, you are not. If you didn't really know who is your father, the head of the *ṭarīqah,* you are misled. Say to that one who is calling you to *ṭarīqah* and misleading you, "You are my brother, not my father. You gave me something, I am happy with it and thank you very much, but you are my brother and I want to find my father. Your shaykh is my father!"

If you don't know their father then they are your brothers; don't be misled, as that will be more balanced. Allāh is saying it's more valuable when you recognize your background and you are going to be forgiven, but you will not be forgiven if you are misled because you have your mind to reason and determine where is your connection.

So with these characteristics, we realize we are not finding that *murshid* between any of these representatives. Of course, Mawlana Shaykh carries not only the level of Murshid at-Tabarruk, but also, as we mentioned from the notes of Grandshaykh and Mawlana Shaykh, the four levels of *irshād* up to Murshid at-Tarbīyyah, the guide of training and raising you up. These characteristics cannot be found except in our spiritual fathers, so don't call yourself *murshid* as you are not yet at that level.

## Knowing the Benefits and Names of All Creation

Then Grandshaykh ق said, Murshid at-Tabarruk has to know all doors of goodness, because it might be what is good for one *murīd* is not good for you. Medicine he takes is good for him but might be poison for you, and what you take is not suitable for him. So Murshid at-Tabarruk must know what specific *dhikr* and *awrād* is best suited for each individual to progress in *ṭarīqah*. He might give everyone something alike at one time, but will assign personalized *tasbīḥ* and practices to individuals. If the *murshid* doesn't know that, he is not in the level of Murshid at-Tabarruk.

He also has to know *abwābu 'l-khayrāt* and *abwābu 'n-ni'am*[3] and all doors of provisions from which Allāh ﷻ will bestow benefit upon you, and he has to know all details of all your sins, major and small. He has to know what his *murīds* have done during that day of good or bad. He has to spiritually reach them immediately if they did not do good, and he will do good on their behalf. If the *murīd* did bad, he will immediately ask forgiveness in the presence of Prophet and Prophet ﷺ asks forgiveness in Allāh's ﷻ Divine Presence for that *murīd* to be forgiven at that moment.

Also, Murshid at-Tabarruk has to inherit that secret knowledge of all names that Allāh ﷻ gave to Sayyīdīnā Adam ﷺ.

> *And He taught Adam all the names (of everything), then He showed them to the angels and said, "Tell Me the names of these if you are truthful."* *Sūratu 'l-Baqara (The Heifer), 2:31*

Today there are huge encyclopedias listing names of everything, with photos and definitions which millions of scientists contribute to. Allāh gave one man, Sayyīdīna Adam ﷺ, knowledge of the entire universe because everything has a name and it cannot exist without a name. Every star in the universe has a name; that star cannot exist without a name. When Allāh taught Adam ﷺ all names, it means everything in *dunyā*, on planets, and throughout the universe, with all their identities and details.

---

[3] Doors of goodness and provision.

Further, you cannot memorize a name without seeing it. I can say to you, "this is a phone" and you repeat, "it is a phone," but immediately you imagine what is the meaning of the phone because you have seen the instrument. So when Allāh ﷻ taught Adam ﷺ the names, he saw what all those names represent; it is not only memorizing names without knowing what it is. Murshid at-Tabarruk inherits from those names.

Mawlana Shaykh, may Allāh grant him long life, says Murshid at-Tabarruk must have the capacity to hold knowledge of the names of everything Allāh created and all specific details relative to them. It is not only that he learned the name of a person, but he can look at that person's face and know what kind of eyes he has, what kind of nose he has. He can differentiate him one person from another, with specific details of every individual, such as how many breaths he will take in a day, in a year, and in all his life.

In addition, Murshid at-Tabarruk has to know every smallest detail of that person: what he is going to feel in his life, how much his heart is pumping every moment. In an Intensive Care Unit (ICU) they connect the patient to machines that monitor his bodily functions until he dies. Murshid at-Tabarruk has to know intimately every detail about you until you leave this *dunyā*.

If you don't see that, don't underestimate the power of *murshid*. These are explanations to understand how difficult *irshād* is and how much Mawlana Shaykh is carrying, with responsibilities that you cannot see in his face. During your entire visit you may personally see Mawlana only five or ten minutes before you leave, and that's all. But you don't know what kind of power and responsibility he is carrying. He is with us, but he is not. He has another image; he has another personality that is always in the presence of Prophet ﷺ. That depends on the level of the *walī*.

Murshid at- Tabarruk has to know everything about you in *dunyā* and what is going to happen to you in *Ākhirah*. And he has to know details about every creature. Allāh said in Holy Qur'an:

> *Until, when they came to the valley of the ants, one of the ants said: "O ants! Enter your dwellings unless Sulaymān and his hosts crush you, while they perceive not.*
>
> *Sūratu 'n-Naml (The Ant), 27:18*

One ant can address all ants without a microphone or speakers; the voice of that ant was able to reach to all ants to warn them the army of Sulaymān is going to step on them, proclaiming, "Oh ants! Run to your cave," meaning, "Run to safety, run to your homes, run to your shaykh, run to Prophet ﷺ, and you will be saved!" And all ants can hear. If one ant is like that, can we speak to people and our voice can reach everyone? That is only for *murshids*. But normal people cannot even reach their egos. That is why Prophet ﷺ said:

> *Man ʿarafa nafsahu, faqad ʿarafa Rabbah.*
> *Who knows himself, knows his Lord.*[4]

---

[4] Allāh said in Sūratu 'ẓ-Ẓārīyāt (51:21), "And also in your own selves, will ye not then see." On this verse, ash-Shaykh Ibrāhīm al-Bājūrī reported the *ḥadīth*, "He who knows himself, knows his Lord." Explaining this *ḥadīth*, he said, "What it means is that he who knows himself is coming into existence and privation, and he knows his Lord by pre-existence and abundance. This is the expoundence of the meaning of the *ḥadīth*. And some say it is an expression of the ineffectiveness of man by saying, 'You don't know yourself, so don't be so advent to claim knowledge of the existence of your Lord.'"
Imām an-Nawawī mentioned something similar in his Fatāwā when asked about this *ḥadīth's* reliability, in which he said, "It is not established, but if it was, when it says, 'he who knows himself', it would mean by his own inability and reliance of his Lord and his worship to Him. And the other part 'he knows his Lord' would mean by His Power and the ability to obliterate creation at His will and His Lordship over all creation."
In the Kashf al-Khafā by Imām ʿAjlūnī, Muḥyīuddīn ibn al-ʿArabī said, "This

Allāh granted Murshid at-Tabarruk to inherit the knowledge of names from Sayyīdīnā Adam ﷺ and Prophet ﷺ. Those who are under his wings or arms has to know them and present them daily to the holy presence of Prophet ﷺ.

## Heavenly Attendants at the Throne of Allāh

Grandshaykh ق said Murshid at-Tabarruk also has to know every bite of food you eat, as Allāh created 300 angels to take it from your mouth through your digestive system, releasing its nourishment. He has to know every angel assigned to you daily, and even if you want to move your finger, there must be an angel sending an inspiration to your mind. Every finger is connected with a different line to the brain; you cannot move your finger if the brain doesn't give an order. You cannot move your eyes, your head, look up, look down without orders from the brain. Murshid at-Tabarruk sees realities of what is going on in the brain. Can we pretend that we are seeing that? No. So if we cannot pretend then we have to know our limits. Your *murshid* has to know about this entire complicated system Allāh gave to our physical beings or he is not yet reaching the level of *irshād*.

That's why Grandshaykh said, "O my shaykh, I don't want that *irshād* if I am not able to bring followers to my level, because for sure they are not going to listen to what I will say and they will run away."

A *ḥadīth* of Prophet ﷺ narrates that during sleep, from the soul of the *mu'min* forty-nine/fiftieths will leave the body, and one-fiftieth will remain with the body to nourish it; the soul goes under Arshullah[5] and makes *sajdah*. As Murshid at-

---

*ḥadīth* is not graded sound by the way of narration, but for us it is sound by the way of *kashf* (unveiling)."

[5] Throne of Allāh ﷻ.

Tabarruk must accompany his *murīds,* he has to know at which moment their soul ascends with Allāh's ﷻ Mercy and Prophet's ﷺ *barakah,* to where it will go, and where it will make *sajdah.*

Murshid at-Tabarruk has to thoroughly know every angel assigned to you day and night, including their names, their characteristics and what they are doing. He has to know all angels that attend his followers and the followers of his other *murshids,* because he has above him three levels: Murshid at-Tazkīyyah, Murshid at-Taṣfīyyah, and Murshid at-Tarbīyyah. So, he has to know every angel by name and what *tasbīḥ* it is making, what favors are written for the followers of that *murshid,* and what honors Allāh ﷻ is bestowing on those *murīds.*

Grandshaykh ق said there are three times in 24 hours that these angels are changing shifts and visit *murīds*: at *imsāk* (*sahūr* time when you stop eating and begin fasting), Ẓuhr time, (middle of the day), and at Maghrib (sunset). Murshid at-Tabarruk has to be present at every shift change, he has to know each angel's replacement angel, what power will come for each *murīd,* for every moment of that day!

## The Direct Connection and Awrad

Murshid at-Tabarruk must have a direct connection; his heart has to be wrapped up and connected by a line all the way to his *murshid,* Murshid at-Tazkīyyah. His *murshid* is Murshid at-Taṣfīyyah, and his *murshid* is Murshid at-Tarbīyyah, the highest level. These four *murshids* are connected to each other. So, Murshid at-Tabarruk has to be connected to his shaykh, and from his shaykh to his shaykh, from his shaykh to his shaykh, from that shaykh to Prophet ﷺ. That connection must always be there; it means any moment he needs anything, it will come. If he has a question the answer comes to his heart without asking, through inspiration. The answer will come from Prophet ﷺ through his shaykh to his heart.

He has to have power from the other three *murshids*. They have been constantly supporting him through his travels, his lectures, his presentations, his advices, and through his *dhikr*. They connect him and send to his heart through a spiritual chain, so he can disperse this to *murīds* and those who come for the first time to listen. This direct connection enables Murshid at-Tabarruk to connect those seekers to his shaykh and from his shaykh to Prophet ﷺ.

The minimum daily *awrād* of Murshid at-Tabarruk is 24,000 *dhikrullāh*. We are doing 1500, 2500, 5000 and sometimes 10,000. In seclusion, sometimes we can go up to 24,000 or 22,000 but he must keep 24,000 throughout the whole day. I remember Grandshaykh ق, said he never saw Mawlana Shaykh Nazim, whom he called "Nazim Effendi," without *tasbīḥ* in his hand. It means he is observing him physically and spiritually. I never saw the *tasbīḥ* drop from his hand.

In the time of Prophet ﷺ there were no beads; they counted on pebbles, and we previously discussed the sunnah of wearing a ring with a stone. The stone is making *dhikrullāh*, which will be written for you as long as it touches your finger. With that *ḥikmah* they order us to wear a ring.

In a *ḥadīth* of Prophet ﷺ, once the pebbles were in the hands of Prophet ﷺ and everyone was hearing their *tasbīḥ*. When Prophet ﷺ put them in Sayyīdīnā Abū Bakr aṣ-Ṣiddīq's ق hand, from his hand to Sayyīdīnā 'Umar's ق hand, then to Sayyīdīnā 'Uthmān's ق hand, and to Sayyīdīnā 'Alī's ق hand, and they were hearing *tasbīḥ*. When the pebbles left Sayyīdīnā 'Alī's hand and were put in the hands of the general *ashāb un-Nabi* ﷺ, no one was hearing *dhikr*, as it is a grant only to certain people.

So, Grandshaykh said, "I never saw Shaykh Nazim Effendi dropping the *tasbīḥ* from his hand." Why, because this is the *shahādah* (index) finger. How do you hold a *tasbīḥ*? You hold it with your *shahādah* finger and your thumb. Why? Because our identity is in the thumb, the fingerprint! No two people have the same fingerprint. It means your ID is encrypted in your thumb.

*Awlīyāullāh* know all about you through your thumb. When they shake your hand or give initiation, you put your hand in their hand and immediately they take all your encrypted information and decode it. Your real identity is what Allāh ﷻ created in His Presence and encrypted in your thumb. So when you say, "*Yā Rabbī,* I am saying *ash-hadu an lā ilāha illa-Llāh wa ash-hadu anna Muḥammadan Rasūlullāh,* I am with my real ID, You are witnessing that I am bringing *shahādah.*" That is why they put these two fingers together. It means wherever you are praising, your *shahādah* finger is witnessing and your ID is presenting it in the presence of Allāh ﷻ.

So that is one of the wisdoms of carrying beads. *awlīyāullāh* encourage us to recite on beads, so our recitation is presented through our reality, not our physicality. Because here is your reality (the thumb). Your reality is taking it to be a witness with your *shahādah* finger, that you are saying, "Allāh ﷻ is the Creator and Sayyīdīnā Muhammad ﷺ is His messenger." Any *dhikr* you recite becomes *ash-hadu an lā ilāha illa-Llāh wa ash-hadu anna Muḥammadan Rasūlullāh.* You say *subḥānAllāh,* it means the same. If you say *shukran lillāh, astaghfirullāh,* whatever you say, they are all working together.

## Make Rabitah to the Shaykh

When you praise Allāh, your praise has a different manifestation at that moment when you are in the Divinely Presence. Many people watch TV doing *dhikrullāh*. I don't want to say don't do that, because many people are doing it, but it's not a perfect way. The perfect way is to keep your heart connected with your shaykh (*rābiṭah*), Murshid at-Tarbīyyah, the highest *murshid*, because *Alḥamdūlillāh*, with Allāh's grace and Prophet's blessings we are connected to the highest level of *irshād,* not Murshid at-Tabarruk, Murshid at-Tazkīyyah or Murshid at-Taṣfīyyah. We are connected in *al-kahf al-Muḥammadi,* the Muhammadan Cave. So, it is more advisable to connect your heart with Mawlana Shaykh and do your *awrād*. (Shaykh Hisham closes his eyes in a contemplative way, and counts on his *tasbīḥ* beads.)

When my brother Shaykh Adnan and I were young, Grandshaykh ق told us to do our *awrād* between 'Aṣr and Maghrib, or between Maghrib and 'Ishā, and half-an-hour or one-hour before Fajr until Ishrāq. He said to make seclusion by covering ourselves with a bed sheet. When you cover yourself you know you are in limitation; this is your *dunyā* grave from which you cannot come out before you finish your *awrād*. We covered as if secluding, disconnecting ourselves from normal life, within that square or rectangle. You cannot move right or left while you are doing your *awrād*. So with that connection to your shaykh, he will take you to the presence of Prophet ﷺ, and from the presence of Prophet he takes you to the presence of Allāh ﷻ.

Murshid at-Tabarruk must have that power or he is not yet reaching Maqām al-Irshād (the Station of Guidance). That's why I say Maqām al-Irshād is not easily acquired, that everyone claims to be a *murshid* of ten, twenty, thirty, one-hundred or two-hundred people. Yes, you can be advising people, giving a lecture that can be accepted or not accepted by people, but the Station of *Irshād* is connecting your *murīds* to the shaykh and to Prophet ﷺ, along with carrying their burdens, their responsibilities, and their liabilities. As soon as you give them *baya*ʿ they are immediately with Mawlana Shaykh, may Allāh give him long life.

Murshid at-Tabarruk has to do at least 24,000 *dhikrullāh* daily and he can go up to 700, 000 *dhikrullāh*. He has to do 24,000 *ṣalawāt* on Prophet ﷺ. This will take at least 3-4 hours. That is the basic *awrād*, to connect, to get his plug, his engine working in order to look after his followers.

So Grandshaykh ق used to say, "I never saw Shaykh Nazim without the beads in his hands, they were all the time in his hands, and I see his lips moving." It's not he had only his beads in his hands but his lips were moving. More than that, when Grandshaykh gave the *ṣuḥbah* in Turkish, and Mawlana Shaykh Nazim was translating it in Arabic. So when Grandshaykh was speaking, Mawlana Shaykh Nazim moved his hands on the beads, moved his lips reciting something, making his *awrād*. As soon as Grandshaykh stopped, it was as if the *dhikr* did not interfere with what he understood of the *ṣuḥbah,* and then he was also translating! Then he stops, Grandshaykh speaks, Mawlana Shaykh Nazim begins another time. I saw that, and his lips were moving. And then Grandshaykh talks, Mawlana Shaykh Nazim takes his beads and he was translating!

Whatever he understood did not interfere with what he was doing and then he was translating every single word, not missing one word. He even said "comma" whenever there was one, for example. To that extent, he doesn't eat too much of the talk. Sometimes translators cannot follow quickly, so they eat much of what is being translated. Mawlana Shaykh never did. The only time he was not holding the *tasbīḥ* was when he went to the bathroom to make *wuḍū*, ablution, then he dropped it. Other than that, his beads were in his hands when he went to bed, when he was sleeping. You can go to his room and see him sleeping with the beads in his hands till today!

Murshid at-Tabarruk is not an easy station. He has to do the *awrād* in order to charge his batteries, his engines. He has to have a spiritual connection so that he will be able to pull, attract his followers, those who are connected to him, and take them up all the way to the other *murshids,* Murshid at-Tazkīyyah, Murshid at-Taṣfīyyah and Murshid at-Tarbīyyah.

## Seventeen Signs on His Face

Grandshaykh ق, says that Allāh gave Murshid at-Tabarruk seventeen different signs you can see in his face. He says, "I didn't explain it because to explain thoroughly I would have to make books on it, so I left it. I was worried about the weak people, because it's such a high level of sainthood that people might deny it, because their hearts are weak and cannot contain the greatness of that *murshid* of the first level."

It means people will come against it and say, "What are you speaking about?" They cannot understand it; it's too high above their level. He said, "I was worried they will fall into *dawratu 'l-inkār,* the circle of denial, because they're not able to understand it. Their minds cannot comprehend what I'm going to say about these seventeen signs. Murshid at-Tarbīyyah has no permission to show anyone and explain to anyone these seventeen signs."

Grandshaykh ق said there is no permission to reveal the seventeen signs and knowledges. Murshid at-Tabarruk has to keep them in his heart until he will be weaned when he reaches Maqām al-Tazkīyyah; only then he has the right to explain the seventeen signs, otherwise he cannot.

We have only discussed the first level of *irshād,* but this will give us an idea of the important of each level. It is not so easy to say, "I am a *murshid.*" People have to know that we are sheep and the shaykh is the shepherd. Anyone who has been given authority to do *dhikr* or bring people to *ṭarīqah* or to Islam did not reach these levels, because they do not possess these characteristics. It is very important to know our limits and not to cross them, or instead of doing good you will begin to do bad, and reflect your sickness on those who follow you, and they might be lost. They will not be responsible: you, who considered yourself a *murshid*, will be held responsible on the Day of Judgment in front of Allāh ﷻ!

For example, if you say, "I'm giving you this money; distribute it," it becomes your responsibility now to distribute it and I'm freed from it. It's now your responsibility to do it and if you don't do it you'll be asked.

## The Traps of Arrogance

It is wise when you give an advice or a presentation to make sure it reaches everyone's heart and that people are not bored by it. Sometimes at seminars or conferences you see people in the audience become sleepy because the presenter speaks in a way that lacks humbleness and he presents himself as a big scholar; his ego is playing with him.

The most dangerous factor in life is our ego, because it always wants to be happy and will always pull you toward the traps of Shayṭān and bad desires. One of the bad desires is arrogance. To think we are so important or famous means we are proud and arrogant. Although you might be struggling against those characters, it is important to understand that mainly our ego always pulls us to be arrogant and with arrogance comes stubbornness, which is very difficult to break through and cut down; it's like a huge cement block that can only be moved with a crane. That's why you need the support of Prophet ﷺ; you need the *wasīlah* (intermediary) which is Sayyīdīnā Muhammad ﷺ and his inheritors.

If that huge obstacle were only a curtain it would be easy to pull it back and pass through, but obstacles created from arrogance and stubbornness are so huge that you cannot accept advice from anyone. However, with the wasīlah, following advice from a true guide crushes that obstacle. Their job and their duty is to remove that obstacle between you and Sayyīdīnā Muhammad ﷺ so you will reach his holy presence through spiritual ways. To reach that sacred station we must not be stubborn or arrogant, because Sayyīdīnā Muhammad ﷺ is the most humble and is teaching us humbleness.

*Alḥamdūlillāh,* Islam came with the divine message carried by Sayyīdīnā Muhammad ﷺ, to take all of us to Allāh's ﷻ Holy Presence. Islam came to move us through these obstacles, but there are many elements in Islam that we are neglecting. Anyone that is a Muslim is doing not everything, but he is doing something, and that is not enough to take away these huge obstacles.

If you are in a tunnel with a lot of obstacles you cannot see and you are told to navigate that tunnel, without a flashlight (torch) you cannot pass through the tunnel. So, Islam has the flashlight and all the elements to remove these difficulties and that flashlight is a true guide, the *murshid* that can show you the way forward. A scholar who did not achieve the level of *murshid* cannot provide such guidance or spiritual openings.

Sayyīdīnā Abdul Qadir al-Jilani ق, a very famous saint in Baghdad and founder of the Qadiri Ṭarīqah, used techniques and methods on his followers that are like a flashlight. He had a very advanced *khalīfah,* to whom the people listened to the extent that you could hear a pin drop. That *khalīfah* had a son who envied his father and how much the *murīds* were captivated by his advice. He thought, "I spent twenty years studying Islam and Shari'ah, and I know more than my father. If they listen to him in such a way, it means when I speak they will be even more attentive and I'll give them knowledge that my father cannot give."

He was looking for an opportunity to speak to the *murīds*. Many people today look for opportunities to speak, so they might claim certain titles such as *khalīfah*, representative, scholar, president, or minister. The father looked into his son's heart and saw the sickness of his ego that he likes to be famous. He said, "Oh my son, today I am ill; you go and give the advice to people." The son was so happy! He was a highly educated scholar, an *ʿalim* , not ignorant like today's representatives of different shaykhs. His father sent him to address the people and he spoke above the knowledge of his father, but one after one, people fell asleep. He was surprised and thought, "I am giving them very deep knowledge that my father never gave." He was opening highly spiritual, mystic knowledge that many *awlīyā* spoke about, but when he spoke, people slept from boredom.

He said to his father, "Oh my father, I experienced something strange today. When I began to speak they slept, but when you speak they open their eyes."

The father answered, "Oh my son, your ego was speaking and I have raised these people against their egos. They will not accept anything coming from ego; they are so sensitive, they can sense it."

Like computerized sensors in a car that monitor performance, those people had sensors in their hearts. If you speak to them something that builds up their ego, their sensors will identify that and they will not listen.

He answered, "Oh my father, I did not say anything to build up their ego. I was giving them some very deep knowledge."

The father answered, "Oh my son, I know you did not speak to build up their ego, but when you opened your mouth that bad smell of the ego made such spots on their hearts, their sensors understood it's full of arrogance, selfishness, and egoism. Also, when you sat in my place you were full of ego, so for sure everyone slept! When I speak I am their shaykh, but I see myself lower than everyone, telling my ego that first I am in need for that advice, more than those I am addressing. You did not do that. You were full of arrogance, and they felt it; that's why they slept. When you speak through your ego people will not pay attention. When you speak through humbleness and declare you are nothing, people will listen."

We might have sicknesses and each of us is struggling to make progress. We come to Mawlana Shaykh Nazim to be uplifted, because to cut down our egos is a continuous struggle. It is not going to end by doing our *awrād*, reading Holy Qur'an, or by praying. We need the *wasīlah*. We are going through life facing temptation. Every day, Shayṭān will come and whisper in our ears and hearts. Every day, there is another problem to face and we are in a continuous struggle against our ego. So we have to declare that first we are in need of what we are saying; we cannot say something to the people and don't apply it to ourselves, or what is the benefit of saying it to the people as you are only cheating them.

You have to apply on yourself first what you like people to hear, then it will be like hitting the target, like a bow shooting an arrow to the center of your heart. If you are not first applying it to yourself but you want others to listen, it's not going to work.

The guides we are speaking about have already applied everything on themselves first. They went through a long struggle to achieve benefit for their students. This is a very, very basic introduction that people must understand. Pride and arrogance are from the seventeen bad characteristics that destroy your advancement. Don't think, "I am an engineer, a professor, an expert… I am better than this one," or "I am this," or "I am that." No. Islam makes everyone equal. Prophet ﷺ said:

*There is no difference between the Arab or non-Arab except in piety.* *Muslim*

This means there is no distinction except through righteousness and sincerity. It means all of us in the eyes of Allāh ﷻ and Prophet ﷺ are equal, as we are all from *Ummat an-Nabī*, the Nation of Prophet ﷺ. Islam grants equality but distinguishes people by their level of sincerity and piety. Someone may be more generous, most educated, most patient, and that one has less anger.

The *murshid* already went through these big struggles and when they speak, they give light to the heart. Like an ignition of the car engine, the *murshid* opens that spark in your heart. That is what is important, because they know how we are. All these guides take from the spiritual tap and give to us.

As Grandshaykh ق wrote in his notes, when he was given the choice to accept *irshād*, he answered, "No, I don't want it, unless you grant that anyone who sits in my *ṣuḥbah* is raised to my level, because I know they are weak servants who are not going to do anything! Shayṭān is after everyone and this life is full of temptations. I do not guarantee they will do their *awrād* or fulfill their religious obligations. I want their love for me to be enough, just as Prophet ﷺ said, 'People will be resurrected with whom they love.' I want those who love me to be granted my level. I will not ask them to do anything because I know they will do it one day and not the next."

There is *barakah* in these holy notes of our sulṭāns. As much as we read them and remind ourselves from their divine wisdom, we take *barakah,* because they have been written by Sulṭān al-Awlīyā Shaykh Sharafuddīn, Sulṭān al-Awlīyā Grandshaykh 'AbdAllāh Fā'iz ad-Dāghestānī, and Sulṭān al-Awlīyā Mawlana Shaykh Nazim al-Haqqani.

May Allāh forgive us, bless us, keep us with our *shuyukh*, with Mawlana Shaykh Nazim, and give him long life and give us long life to see Mahdī.

*Wa min Allāhi 't-tawfiq, bi ḥurmati 'l-ḥabīb, bi ḥurmati 'l-Fātiḥah.*
*And with Allāh is success. For the sake of the Beloved, for his sake we recite the opening chapter of Holy Qur'an.*

# Murshid at-Tazkiyyah: Guide of Purification

*Madad yā Sulṭān al-Awlīyā, Shaykh Muḥammad Nāẓim al-Ḥaqqānī.*
*Madad yā Sulṭān al-Awlīyā, Shaykh 'AbdAllāh al-Fā'iz ad-Dāghestānī.*

A train runs on a track to reach its destination. There is the main track and side tracks, and the main destiny is the straight-forward track. Sometimes tracks have diversions that take the train away from the main track, for turning or to enter another designated track, then the diversion closes and you return to the main track. So really there is only one track.

Our track is Mawlana Shaykh Nazim al-Haqqani, may Allāh give him long life. Anyone who is on his train will go straight-forward and be saved, but he has to be on the main track. If he diverts he will find a dead-end and will have to return to the main track.

The train has one engine but many wagons. You can jump on any wagon to reach your destination. If you are in the first, second or third wagon, you would be so near to the main engine that you can see what the engineer is doing. If you are in the last wagon you don't see much, but you will be pulled wherever the train is going. With luck you'll be in the first, second, or third wagon. Who has luck but not as much as the first three, is still pulled along by the train and will reach their destination.

Murshid at-Tazkīyyah, the Guide of Purification, is the second level of *irshād,* one level above Murshid at-Tabarruk. He has achieved all the levels of Murshid at-Tabarruk and has put his feet on Maqām al-Tazkīyyah. "Purification" means to give you a hint, or a jump-start. He is a means to make the vehicle of your heart to move.

What are the characteristics of Murshid at-Tazkīyyah? Many *ṭarīqahs* insist on these issues because they are important. Grandshaykh ق says, Murshid at-Tazkīyyah purifies your heart. He must keep the Sharīʿah at every moment, according to the four Islamic schools of thought. He must have complete comprehension of all the four schools: Hanafi, Maliki, Shafiʿi and Hanbali. He has to maintain his faith and practices according to teachings of Imām Abū Hanīfa, Imām Malik, Imām Shafiʿi, and Imām Hanbul. He must first apply that knowledge to himself, then to people around him.

Murshid at-Tazkīyyah must be able to give a *fatwa*[6] on any issue as decided within these four schools. He must not leave even one of what Prophet ﷺ was ordered by Allāh ﷻ of the 500 obligations and 800 forbiddens. He must not have any kind of bad inspirations or gossips in his heart, which must always get inspirations to benefit him, his *murīds*, and Ummat an-Nabi ﷺ.

As part of his daily *awrād* he must do at least 24,000 *dhikrullāh* and 24,000 *ṣalawāt*. In addition, he is responsible to put on the tongues of his *murīds* both *dhikrullāh* and *ṣalawāt*, as if they have recited 24,000 *dhikrullāh* and 24,000 *ṣalawāt*, which he will do on their behalf daily. If he has 1,000 *murīds*, he must do it 1,000 times, multiplied by 24,000 *dhikrullāh* and 24,000 *ṣalawāt!*

Grandshaykh further explains that Allāh ﷻ gives *awlīyāullāh* not an analog tongue, but a digital tongue with a very acute, sharp wavelength that can recite quickly, what is known in Arabic as *tayy* (folding).

> *The Day that We roll up the heavens like a scroll rolled up for books (completed); even as We produced the first creation, so shall We produce a new one; a promise We have undertaken. Truly shall We fulfill it.* *Sūratu 'l-Anbīyā, 21:104*

---

[6] Legal ruling based on the highest levels of Islamic jurisprudence.

Allāh ﷻ said, "I am going to fold it, to close it, like We close a book." It means this whole space will shrink to something small. Allāh ﷻ is giving the example of folding a book; the tongue can have this power as it will be folded. Like airplanes moving through space; space is folded and time is shrunk, but still you are moving fast enough to reach your destination. Let's say you are in America and you want to go to Cyprus, which previously took 90 days by boat, but today you reach it in 20 hours. You are shrinking the time, but not shrinking the space; still you are able to go in space. Similarly, *awlīyāullāh* have the power to shrink their tongue to do a huge number of *dhikr* in very short time.

Murshid at-Tazkīyyah has to put this *awrād* as if his *murīd* did it. When the shaykh does it on behalf of the *murīd* it has no ego, no arrogance, no pride: it is pure. Because of that pure *dhikr*, when we say *Allāhu akbar*, we become clean as if he cleaned your heart. When you are clean, you are in Allāh's Presence, but when you are dirty, you cannot be in that Presence.

That's why in prayer you must be clean, praying on a carpet, or on sand in the desert, or in a forest, on cement, even on grass, it has to be clean, it has to be clean, it has to be clean! You cannot pray where there is litter or impurities. When you make physical ablution you can then pray. With *dhikrullāh* and *ṣalawāt* on Prophet ﷺ, *awlīyāullāh* give us a spiritual ablution. Murshid at-Tazkīyyah is authorized to do that. He has been authorized to call upon any *walī* in the Naqshbandi Sufi Order, living or non-living. If he wants to call on Mawlana Shaykh Nazim, who is Sulṭān al-Awlīyā, who is Murshid at-Tarbīyyah, the highest level of *irshād*, he can call and get the answer. If he wants to call on those who left *dunyā*, he can reach them in the grave.

Murshid at-Tazkīyyah can call upon any *walī*, and there might be 100 *walīs* in the level of Murshid at-Tabarruk, and

1,000 or even 10,000 *walīs* in the level of Murshid at-Tazkīyyah; we don't know their numbers, but he can reach them all. Of the 124,000 *walīs* on Earth, at all times there are 7,007 living saints of the Naqshbandi Sufi Order. Murshid at-Tazkīyyah can reach any of them in any moment, to get answers or to take energy from them, whether they are alive or in their graves.

Allāh ﷻ releases the spirit of a *mu'min* so he can move around and his grave will be a small paradise for him until the Day of Judgment. This applies particularly to those about whom Prophet ﷺ said in a *Ḥadīth Qudsī* reported by Imām Ghazālī; Hujwirī:

*My saints are under My domes; no one knows them except Me.*

They have power to know, hear, and contact saints in their graves. We hope Allāh ﷻ releases our souls in our graves and makes them a small paradise for us, also!

Murshid at-Tazkīyyah has power over the four enemies, who are very aggressive against human beings: *nafs, dunyā, hawā* and Shayṭān. *Nafs* is the self, *dunyā* is the materialistic world, *hawā* is bad desires, and Shayṭān. Those four enemies are always after us in this life, they chase everyone and try to destroy their relationship with Prophet ﷺ and Allāh ﷻ.

So as I said before, I am concentrating on these four important levels of guides, because today too many misunderstand the meaning of *murshid*. Everyone is calling himself *murshid*, from the Far West to Far East. So we are trying to focus on what Grandshaykh 'AbdAllāh, Shaykh Sharafuddīn, and Mawlana Shaykh Nazim said about this issue in their notes.

Murshid at-Tazkīyyah has the power to purify every *murīd* connected with him. He can reach them, purify them, and stop the aggression of these four enemies. Whatever they have done during the day and night against his *murīds*, to ensure there is no sin left on his *murīds*, he changes *sayyīāt* (bad deeds) to *ḥasanāt* (good deeds) by taking them to Prophet's ﷺ door through Murshid at-Taṣfīyyah and Murshid at-Tarbīyyah, the guides above his station. This is one of the meanings of the *āyah* Allāh ﷻ revealed to Sayyīdinā Muhammad ﷺ:

> *When they were unjust to themselves, had they come to you and begged Allāh's Forgiveness, and the Messenger had begged forgiveness for them, indeed, they would have found Allāh All-Forgiving, Most Merciful.* *Sūratu 'n-Nisā (The Women), 4:64*

When someone has done something wrong he is taken to court, where a defense attorney will present his case and the judge will listen to his legal argument. Similarly, Murshid at-Tazkīyyah will take his *murīds* to the presence of Prophet ﷺ, and ask him to make *istighfār* on their behalf, as Allāh ﷻ said, "When they are oppressors to themselves they come to you, yā Muhammad. They ask Allāh's forgiveness and you have to ask on their behalf forgiveness."

So when that *murshid* brings his *murīds* there, he makes them to say *istighfār* through their hearts in the presence of Prophet ﷺ, who will do *istighfār* on their behalf and, "They will find Allāh ﷻ forgiving their sins." Mawlana Shaykh, may Allāh give him long life, and Grandshaykh ق, said Allāh forgives all your sins. I heard it, I learned it, I know it, I witnessed many times Grandshaykh saying all sins, even *kaba'ir* will be forgiven, because Prophet ﷺ said, "*My shafa'ah* (intercession) *is for those who commit the grave sins.*" It means any sinner can repent and Allāh ﷻ will forgive them. However, there is one sin Allāh will never forgive, which is very important for us to know and very difficult for *awlīyā* to carry.

## Consequences of Backbiting and Breaking Hearts

Grandshaykh ق said, "Our door is open so wide from East to West for anyone to come and repent, and we will find such a way for them that even if they want to go out they cannot, as our door will close to keep them inside that mercy! There is only one sin that we are not allowed to defend, although they will petition us to seek forgiveness on their behalf."

This is based on the *ḥadīth* of the two *Ṣaḥābah* who came to Prophet ﷺ one morning and said, *"Yā Rasūlullāh,* we have a stomach ache that is tearing our stomachs apart!" Prophet ﷺ said, "Today you ate raw meat." They answered, *"Yā Rasūlullāh,* we did not see meat for a long time." Prophet ﷺ said, "No, this morning you ate raw meat; put your fingers in your throat and vomit." They said, *"Yā Rasūlullāh,* we didn't eat meat." He ﷺ again told them they ate meat and to vomit. When they did, there was raw meat with blood oozing out of it. Prophet ﷺ is the doctor of the *Ummah,* who can see the illnesses in everyone. Astonished, they said, *"Yā Rasūlullāh, w'Allāhi* (by Allāh), we didn't eat meat!" He said, "You did backbite (spread confusion against) your brother."

Backbiting is the biggest sin that has no remedy. Because when you sin and repent, that is between you and Allāh and Allāh will forgive you. But when you backbite someone, it becomes between you and that person, so you must apologize and ask him to forgive you. If he does not forgive you, that sin is not erased! Then on the Day of Judgment, the victims of backbiting seek justice from Allāh.

That is why Prophet ﷺ asked the *Ṣaḥābah* ؓ, "Who is bankrupt?" They answered, *"Yā Rasūlullāh,* the one who doesn't have money." Prophet ﷺ answered, "No, the one who is bankrupt is he who has no good *'amal."* They asked, *"Yā Rasūlullāh,* even if he prays and fasts he has no good *'amal*? What happened to his prayers and fasting?" Prophet ﷺ

answered, "They are gone, because he did backbite his brother."

Those who were backbitten, about whom people spread confusion, will take their rights from Allāh ﷻ. On the Day of Judgment, Allāh will bring the oppressor to whom they oppressed and say, "O My servant (the oppressed), do you forgive him?" The oppressed will answer, "No, *yā Rabbī*. He spoke very badly about me in *dunyā* and created a lot of *fitna*. I will not forgive him! I want my rights from him!" And Allāh ﷻ will say, "This is your brother in Islam." He will again reply, "*Yā Rabbī*, I'm not accepting, I want my rights."

If it was a sin between Allāh and that person He will forgive, but because of the "right of servants" (*ḥuqūq 'l-ʿībād*), people will have rights on each other and it is Allāh's ﷻ duty to restore justice. So He will give the *ḥasanāt* of the oppressor to the one he oppressed. Allāh ﷻ will then ask, "Are you satisfied?" The oppressed will answer, "Not yet, *yā Rabbī*! He did a lot to me!" Allāh will continue giving the oppressor's good deeds, his prayers and his fasting, until he has nothing left, and the oppressed one will say, "*Yā Rabbī*, I'm not finished yet, he did a lot against me!" And Allāh knows these persons did against each other a lot. And at the end He will begin to take from the *sayyīāt* of the oppressed and give to the oppressor, until the oppressed is satisfied and says, "*Yā Rabbī*! I am satisfied." Allāh says, "Okay, you go to Paradise." So what did the oppressor end up with? No *ḥasanāt* and more *sayyiʿat*.

People are going to take their rights on the Day of Judgment. I have rights against many people because they spread confusion about me. I am going to take my rights, not in *dunyā*, I don't want it in *dunyā* as it doesn't mean anything. I am going to ask Allāh to give it to me in *Ākhirah*. I am holding these people responsible and liable. I am not forgiving them, anyone who said against me one word I am asking Allāh ﷻ on the Day of Judgment to give my rights from these people and I am holding them responsible. They know themselves and they know what they have done.

Murshid at-Tazkīyyah is the one trying to take all the four enemies away from the *murīds*, but he will be stuck with one thing: when someone has been backbitten, he cannot repair that. That person will ask Allāh on the Day of Judgment to take his rights from the one who backbited him. I'm quoting Grandshaykh ق; ask anyone in his time and he will tell you that Grandshaykh ق said, "There is forgiveness for any sin, Allāh will forgive. Even if anyone becomes a *munāfiq* (hypocrite) I will find a way for him to repent. But I cannot carry anyone that broke the heart of someone on Earth. Any human being, any background, breaking hearts of people is not accepted in Islam. I will not and cannot, and I don't like to see from my *murīds* anyone who breaks the heart of another."

Breaking hearts how? When you backbite people, when you said *ghībah* (backbiting), *namīmah* (slander), and *fitna* (confusion), for what, for *dunyā* issues? Trying to separate brothers from each other, sisters from each other, husband and wife from each other? What's your benefit? You think you get nearer to that one? Don't you know that blood cannot be separated?

Those who are carrying the blood of Prophet ﷺ, inheritors of Prophet, or the grandchildren of Prophet, don't try to put your fingers there! You cannot split them, you cannot separate them. They will still be brothers, they will still be sisters, and they will still be parents. You cannot split and separate. I am speaking to these cameras here. Those people who they are trying to separate people from each other, spreading confusion, know themselves.

Grandshaykh ق said breaking the heart of any human being is not accepted. All doors are open except to the one that is breaking the heart of someone else. Today the *Ummah* is falling into this problem of everyone breaking the heart of the other. So as Mawlana Shaykh Nazim's *murīds* we have to be one and there has to be unity.

## Confusion in Our Ranks

There are a lot of people who want to see this Sufi Order go down and the problem is not coming from outside, it is coming from inside. I don't like to speak on these issues but today it is opened up. In every Sufi Order there are people from within who try to split the whole *ṭarīqah,* and for what? What is the benefit? They claim, "This is the inner circle, this is the outer circle, this *murīd* is closest to the shaykh, this one is the best *murīd,* this one is not the best." What is the benefit?

So they plant their allies within the group and recruit others to make circles, to destroy the *ṭarīqah* from within. I pity them, because Shayṭān is playing with them! We are speaking about Murshid at-Tazkīyyah, we are trying to teach from Mawlana Shaykh's and Grandshaykh's teachings for us to benefit. Grandshaykh ق said whenever someone sits in our association, whatever *walī* we speak about, they will reach that level. This is not our association, it is Mawlana's association and everyone here is being respected by Mawlana Shaykh! So we have to be united, and we must not try to split each other. I am not only speaking about Mawlana Shaykh's place in Lefke, Cyprus, but also what is happening around the world!

We are running from one place to bring more people to *ṭarīqah,* and to raise the name of Mawlana Shaykh higher. Show me around the world what they have done for Mawlana Shaykh. They are in small circles of 10, 15, 20, 30, 50, 100, or 200 people. They claim to be a *murshid* and become a VIP who goes to clubs and discos! Instead of bringing everyone together on one heart and supporting those who are trying their best and running from one place to another, those people have nothing but backbiting for others.

In Indonesia there are *mashāAllāh* tens of thousands of *murīds*, millions who have *baya*ʿ with Mawlana Shaykh Nazim, not with me, although I represented Mawlana Shaykh in Indonesia since 1997. In 2009, in a big gathering of 250,000 people in Jakarta's Masjid al-Istiqlal, the president of Indonesia announced he is a student of this *ṭarīqah*. We are trying our best to spread the teachings, but some people stab us in the back, and for what? This is *ṭarīqah*? This is Islam? No. I can name them, but it is not necessary. We leave them for Allāh ﷻ and His Prophet ﷺ to judge. Those same people come to Mawlana Shaykh Nazim, saying, "*Yā Sayyīdī*, oh please, we love you," and they show themselves as very close to Mawlana Shaykh. *Alḥamdūlillāh*, you show you are very close to Mawlana Shaykh, but don't stab others in the back!

We are happy to see more people coming to this *ṭarīqah*, not fewer people. I not only have permission from Mawlana Shaykh Nazim and Grandshaykh to teach, I am also Mawlana Shaykh Nazim's son-in-law. If you don't want to respect that permission, *ijāzah*, from Grandshaykh and Mawlana Shaykh, at least respect that I am his son-in-law! I am sorry to say this. This is being broadcast live around the world, and I don't want to say who these people are, but you can count them! In Europe a little bit here and there, in America a little bit, in Malaysia a little bit, I didn't see in Indonesia, in the Middle East, in UK, in Europe there are people making *fitna* among *murīds*. May Allāh ﷻ forgive them and forgive us.

Why did I say I am going to take my rights on the Day of Judgment? I am forgiving them, no problem. Those who slander me are Mawlana's *murīds* and they love Mawlana, so what do we want better? If we forgive, Allāh ﷻ will forgive us, because we also have a lot of sins. May Allāh forgive us and forgive them. It's okay, we are still brothers and sisters; we cannot run away from them. We have one father, our shaykh, Mawlana Shaykh Muhammad Nazim Adil al-Haqqani, and our grandfather is Grandshaykh 'AbdAllāh al-Fā'iz ad-Dāghestānī.

My paternal and maternal grandfathers are descendants of Sayyīdinā al-Ḥasan and Sayyīdinā al-Ḥusayn, from Prophet ﷺ. Me and my brother, Shaykh Adnan, do not come from garbage!

Once Grandshaykh ق called us into a private room in his house, and I am narrating it in public now with no translator. Mawlana Shaykh Nazim was in Cyprus. This happened in 1970, when many of you were not yet born. Grandshaykh gave me and my brother a one-hour *ṣuḥbah,* and I will not mention everything. He said to us, "Allāh ﷻ gave me you and your brother like a bean." Grandshaykh liked to eat red beans and he often cooked them himself. He said, "Allāh gave you both to me like a bean split into two identical halves. A bean without the other part cannot exist; it must have the two parts together. You complete each other."

So this is what I want to tell you: after he elaborated on many different issues that I cannot speak, he said, "To me and in the holy presence of Prophet ﷺ you two will always be together."

There are people today who try to cut that. I am speaking to them now, informing them that my brother and I will never be separated! I am happy to be under his feet! We were two from the family. We will never forget the days we spent, since the first time we visited Grandshaykh in 1958! And now newcomers who don't know this history are asking, "What is your business? Who appointed you?"

May Allāh ﷻ forgive us and forgive them.

## Laziness Blocks Higher Levels of Knowledge

The *murshid* tries as much as he can to clean his followers. The baby needs his diaper changed frequently; similarly, a *murshid* frequently changes our dirty character by asking Allāh ﷻ on our behalf to forgive us through Prophet's intermediation. Murshid at-Tazkīyyah eliminates the dirty character of laziness from those connected to him. We are lazy. They ask us to recite 10,000 *dhikrullāh* and we recite five; they ask us recite five and we do 1000; they ask us recite 1000 and we don't do anything! We are created to be like that.

When Prophet ﷺ ascended in Laylat al-Isrāʿ wa'l-Miʿrāj (the Night Journey and Ascension), Allāh ﷻ ordered him to tell his *Ummah* to pray 50 times daily. Sayyīdīna Mūsā ﷺ asked, "*Yā* Muhammad ﷺ! What did Allāh give you as prayer obligations? Be careful, because I know whatever I asked Bani Israel to do they were lazy, so ask less!" So Prophet ﷺ asked less until the obligation was 45 prayers, but Sayyīdīna Mūsā ﷺ kept telling him to ask for less, until Allāh lowered the daily obligation to five prayers. Then Sayyīdīna Mūsā ﷺ told him: "*Yā* Muhammad ﷺ! Ask less, I know they are not even going to pray the five prayers." Prophet answered, "I feel shy from my Lord." About this Allāh ﷻ replied, "*Yā* Muhammad ﷺ, it is five, but on the Scale of Deeds it is 50 (one *ḥasanāt* multiplied by ten). I'm giving them ten rewards for every prayer."

When *awlīyāullāh* order us to do something, Shayṭān is behind us. We are lazy, we don't do it and we run away. Murshid at-Tazkīyyah has the power of removing that laziness from his followers. Shayṭān tries his best to keep us lazy, but that *murshid* is trying his best to pull us from laziness. To encourage us not to follow Shayṭān, his talks and advice is often about the traps of Shayṭān. Today, Mawlana Shaykh, may Allāh give him long life, often speaks against Shayṭān because he is treating us at that first level. He's not treating us at the highest level and that's why we see today, even so many years after Grandshaykh's time, Mawlana Shaykh's lectures, talks and advice are from the level of ego—against ego, against Shayṭān, against the four enemies—because he wants to make sure that we are clear from them so that we can rise up to listen. Still we are not listening! *Wa qālū samiʿnā wa aṭaʿnā,* "They say, '*Yā Rabbī*! We heard and we obeyed!" When we reach that level, when we say we listened and obeyed, then at that time they can give us from the highest level of knowledge.

Now all talks are about very basic spirituality. If I go through this notebook of Grandshaykh ق, you'd be amazed about what they speak! It's beyond limits of the human mind. That's why the level of *awlīyā* is very high and we cannot understand them. That's why so many times the people came against *awlīyāullāh,* as their speaking was so high above the general knowledge of their time. These days, Mawlana only speaks at the lower levels of knowledge, according to our understanding.

Grandshaykh ق said, Murshid at-Tazkīyyah purifies his followers from laziness, and from feeling cold toward *ṭarīqah,* and from feeling warm toward bad desires; he purifies their hearts to feel cold toward bad desires and warm toward heavenly desires. The most important thing is, Murshid at-Tazkīyyah must take away from their minds hallucinations and illusions.

Today many people cannot be basic; they hallucinate and follow illusions that exist only in their minds. They say true *taṣawwuf* is to be in a journey of *maʿrifatullāh*. If you are still wearing a diaper, how can you know Allāh ﷻ? No one knows Allāh; they only know about His Beautiful Names and Attributes. Before you know *maʿrifatullāh,* you have to know yourself, as it is said, *man ʿarafa nafsahu faqad ʿarafa rabbahu,* "Who knows himself, knows his Lord."

What is the benefit of a guide teaching you from Unseen knowledge that he has seen but you have not? What are you going to understand? It will make you more lazy. There are people who admire a shaykh who speaks from very high knowledge, but how does that benefit you if you are not praying the five prayers, if you are not doing the basics of Islam, if you don't call for unity, if you don't bring people together, if you don't build your community and help them through your business, your work, your donation, your generosity? What is the benefit of going up high and seeing the penthouse? You don't have the money to buy or lease the penthouse or rent it, so what is the benefit to look at it? Look at those below you, then you will appreciate what you have.

Grandshaykh ق and Mawlana Shaykh, may Allāh give him long life, gave me direct permission, *ijāzah,* to teach spirituality and they have sent me East and West. What I realized very early in my travels is, what is the benefit to speak from a high level of knowledge when people are still in Kindergarten? If someone puts a turban on their head and grows a long beard, they say, "We are wearing like *sunnah* of Prophet." But *sunnah* is to wear something loose. In reality, Prophet ﷺ wore a *thawb*, a full-length *qamīṣ*. I met many people calling themselves Naqshbandī, Rifaʿī, Qādirī, Burhānī, Qarībī, Shādhilī, who follow only what is being described as spirituality and they don't even pray! So what's the benefit? I found it is better to talk about Sharīʿah teachings as they will not understand even basic principles of *ṭarīqah*.

You need to apply the Sharīʿah first before going to Ḥaqīqah. Prophet came with Sharīʿah, first with the five obligations, the five pillars of Islam, then with the six levels of Iman: your *ʿaqīdah*. You have to learn your *ʿaqīdah* first. Do you know what is your *ʿaqīdah*? If I ask this question, I'm 100% sure no one can answer. *ʿaqīdah* is our belief, how we believe in Allāh's Oneness. It is a basic question in Islamic Sharīʿah. Many

Muslims don't know that Prophet ﷺ came with five obligatory pillars of Islam, six pillars of *imān*, and the highest level of moral excellence *(iḥsān)*. It's the highest level of spirituality of *tazkīyyat an-nafs*, "purification of the self." Master these, then you are able to understand!

## Sultan Salim and Muhiyuddin Ibn al-Arabi

The people executed Sayyīdīna Muḥīyiddīn Ibn al-'Arabī ق, because they didn't understand the high knowledge from which he spoke. Even some scholars said, "Muḥīyiddīn Ibn al-'Arabī did something wrong, so we hanged him." What he did wrong? What he wrote in his books? Finally he said to the people, "What you worship is under my feet (Your god is under my feet." So they got upset; like today there are scholars who don't understand what is *ṭarīqah, Ḥaqīqah,* Sharī'ah. They say, "*Ṭarīqah* is bad, so we must question those who follow it." They send questions at a Kindergarten level, the meaning of which they don't know! In Malaysia today, they are asking for someone to answer questions about *ṭarīqah,* because all their knowledge is basic. They cannot go beyond their minds. That's why it is useless to speak to such people about *ṭarīqah.*

In his esteemed book al-Futuhat al-Makiyyah, Shaykh Muḥīyiddīn Ibn al-'Arabī ق wrote, "The secret of Muḥīyiddīn Ibn al-'Arabī cannot be known until the *sīn* enters the *shīn.*" [7] So they hanged him. They are not going to understand what he's talking about, and you will confuse people if you speak to them from high levels and say they are *kāfir* (unbeliever). There is no benefit in that, so speak normally, from basic teachings.

They hanged Muhiyuddīn Ibn 'Arabi ق and threw his body in a dump. They didn't even bury him because they said

---

[7] Letters of the Arabic alphabet.

he is *murtād* (apostate). They said this about one of the biggest saints of Islam!

Sulṭān Salīm, the Ottoman Emperor, came to Turkey and invaded Damascus, known in Arabic as "Sham." "Salīm" is spelled with the Arabic letter *sīn*, and "Sham" is spelled with the Arabic letter *shīn*. Sulṭān Salīm took Sham from the hands of the unbelievers, and it became the holy city of Damascus. Prophet Muhammad ﷺ gave more than forty *ḥadīth*s on the "arrow of Sham," because according to the *ḥadīth* of Prophet, Allāh's throne will descend in that area. That's why Sayyīdīna ʿIsa ﷺ will descend on the white minaret of Masjid al-Umawīyyahin Damascus, where many *Ahlu'l-Bayt* and *Ṣaḥābah* ﷺ are buried.

So when Sulṭān Salīm entered, he ordered his army to prepare for him the Turkish bath. You know at that time they had a huge area they used as a bathhouse, with bathtubs like steam saunas. Sulṭān Salīm entered and saw a vision[8] of someone sitting in his bath.

That one said, "*Yā* Salīm!" The *sulṭān* was stunned that someone would address him by his first name. He knew no one could pass his security guards without his knowledge, and he was frightened. Even the bathtub trembled with fear!

That one said, "*Yā* Salīm, rub my back!"

Sulṭān Salīm rubbed that one's back, and he said, "*Yā* Salīm, I wrote in my books that my secrets will come out when the *sīn* enters the *shīn*. It is written in the Preserved Tablet that today my secret will appear. I am Muḥīyiddīn Ibn al-ʿArabī . I was executed based on false rumors. I've been backbited, backbited, backbited!"

---

[8] Some prefer to say it is a "vision"; however, *ṭarīqah* holds that *awlīyāullāh* experience events in other dimensions as a reality.

If people are backbitten for one year, some begin to believe it, then it becomes a legend and they build on it. They don't know from the beginning that it was wrong. They embellish facts based on what they've heard from one generation to another. They don't know truth from falsehood; they think the legend is reality. That's why Prophet ﷺ prohibited backbiting, spreading confusions and false rumors, which are great sins.

Through malicious gossip and backbiting, the people killed Muhiyuddin Ibn 'Arabi ق. Don't kill your brothers with your backbiting! Repent and Allāh will forgive you. Have the courage to repent and ask for forgiveness from the ones you have backbitten; I am telling myself and everyone. Have the courage to apologize to them, then it will be finished. To be cleared up here is better than to be punished in the Hellfire.

Sulṭān Salīm answered him, "Is your secret to be revealed tonight? How am I going to know where you are buried?"

Muhiyuddin Ibn 'Arabi ق answered, "First, take me out of my place where they threw me."

This event occurred 300 years later, not a few years later. He is saying to take him from where he is still existing, his remaining skeleton. Sulṭān Salīm wondered how to find him?

Muhiyuddin Ibn 'Arabi ق instructed him, "Go to Masjid al- Umawīyyah in Damascus."

That famous site was sacred to both Christians and Jews. When Sayyīdīna 'Umar ؓ entered Damascus and prayed there, he modified the site to accommodate worshippers from all three faiths. He established the mosque for the Muslims to pray on one side so as not disturb anyone, and for the Jews and Christians to pray unhindered in their places. Sayyīdīna 'Umar ؓ was a just *khalīfah*; he did not stop non-Muslims from worshipping. That's why Masjid al-Umawīyyah is a sacred site that holds many spiritual secrets.

Muhiyuddin Ibn ʿArabi ق said, "You will see light coming from the Earth up to the sky. Follow that light to where it comes."

Sulṭān Salīm went with his army to the origin of the light, from the top of the hill to the bottom, and he saw the source of that light. They found a dump where people had thrown garbage for countless years, until it decomposed. He ordered his army to haul it away and they dug down seventy to eighty meters, where eventually, amidst the horrific, rotten smell came a magnificent, lovely fragrance. There they uncovered a shroud and inside was the fresh, undecayed body of Muhiyuddin Ibn ʿArabi ق. His skin was fresh and intact, and his face was still pink and lovely!

Sulṭān Salīm and his army immediately removed Muhiyuddin Ibn ʿArabi ق to a fresh grave they dug, around which the *sulṭān* ordered his holy *maqām* to be built. That site is Masjid al-Muhiyuddin Ibn al-ʿArabi, the world-renowned mosque built by Sulṭān Salīm of the Ottoman Empire to honor that famous *walī* 300 years after his execution!

But he did not stop at that; he wanted to check. He said, "For this terrible injustice, I want to kill all those *ʿulamā* and their descendants! I want to see the reality of what happened." They found someone 137 years old, from whom Sulṭān Salīm asked, "O my father, do you remember anything about Muḥīyiddīn Ibn al-ʿArabī , what he said, or where he was killed?" That aged man answered, "*Yā Sayyīdī*, I remember that my father who also lived 100 years told me that his grandfather told him that they killed Muḥīyiddīn Ibn al-ʿArabī ق on this spot. And my father showed me this place that his father showed him. His father said Muḥīyiddīn Ibn al-ʿArabī was executed because he told a crowd of people, "What you worship is under my feet," so they hanged him in the same place. That aged man took Sulṭān Salīm to the place of execution, which happened to be near where they buried him, which is now Masjid al-Muhiyuddin Ibn al-'Arabi.

The army dug a huge hole like a well going three-to-four meters down, where they found seven barrels of gold coins from olden times. It means Muhiyuddin Ibn 'Arabi ق was telling them, "What you worship is that *dunyā* under my feet! I don't worship what you worship! I worship Allāh ﷻ!"

They didn't understand and they backbited him. You see where backbiting took them? It ended up in a wrongful killing. That's why today *awlīyāullāh* don't speak from high levels of knowledge, but if they do, they must be at a high level. Sometimes when we are upstairs with Mawlana Shaykh in his private room, he speaks a very high *ṣuḥbah* in Arabic, which cannot be posted because others can't understand it and it would cause problems. The problem is not with Mawlana Shaykh; he doesn't care. The problem is with us, that we cannot understand!

So backbiting is dangerous. Some people say, "Why don't you speak from high knowledge?" One time we spoke something and they printed a book from what we spoke that caused *fitna*, confusion. This issue is constantly being brought up. I tried to defend it but we could not, so in the end I left the issue alone. You cannot speak from higher stations because people don't understand it so they backbite you. Until today they are backbiting on the Internet what has been published by some people. Backbiting is not good.

I'll tell you a story that affects some converts. In 1995, a Buddhist and his mother, who was also Buddhist, converted to Islam and became very dedicated students. He got married and was teaching, and then he asked to set up a place to attend prayer and hold *dhikr*. I saw him some time later not happy, saying he doesn't want to hold *dhikr* in that place any longer.

He said, "Many things came to my ear, all kinds of garbage, and now I am asking not to have any relationship with you."

He may have been brainwashed by the poisonous gossip of those who spread *fitna*. Allah will take back our rights.

Help people come together. All *awlīyā* have been criticized; Grandshaykh ق was taken to court because he said something that people quoted out of context.

A divine curse comes on backbiters and the stench of badness accompanies them in their grave! Be careful from stories; even if they are true, don't spread them around and contaminate others.

## Be Purified through Your Sadaqa

*Alḥamdūlillāh,* we are blessed to be from the nation of Muhammad ﷺ and to receive the divine guidance Allāh ﷻ bestows on His Prophet ﷺ, and what Prophet gives to hearts of *awlīyāullāh.*

> *Obey Allāh, obey Prophet ﷺ and obey those who are on authority.* *Sūratu 'n-Nisā (The Women), 4:59*

> *And whatever the Messenger gives you, take it, and whatever he forbids you, abstain and fear Allāh. Verily, Allāh is severe in punishment.* *Sūratu 'l-Ḥashr (The Banishment), 59:7*

> *Prophet ﷺ said, "Ḥalāl (permissible) is very clear like sunshine, and ḥarām (forbidden) is very clear like sunshine."* *Bukhārī*

You cannot mix the two: either you are on the side of *ḥalāl* or you are on the side of *ḥarām*. We cannot take a little bit from *ḥalāl* or a little bit of *ḥarām,* and if by mistake or by a sin you did something *ḥarām,* you have to repent. We are not saying that people will ever be perfect and will not commit any sin. No, people are weak. We are weak servants to Allāh ﷻ; we are helpless and heedless.

We must know that whatever wrong we do, immediately we must repent, because at that moment the power of the *murshid* comes. Don't think the *murshid* is heedless! He must give to you to show you your heedlessness—he has power. There are people who consider themselves *murshid* but by name only. In the time of Prophet ﷺ, *tasawwuf*[9] was a reality but had no name, and today it is a name with no reality. The state of *tazkīyyat an-nafs*, "purification of the soul" is mentioned in Holy Qur'an:

> *Khudh min amwālihim ṣadaqatan tuṭāhhirūḥ um wa tuzakkīhim bihā wa ṣalli ʿalayhim inna ṣalātaka sakanun lahum w'Allāhu Samīʿun ʿAlīm.*
> *Of their goods take alms that you might purify and sanctify them; and pray on their behalf. Verily, your prayers are a source of security for them. And Allāh is All-Hearing, All-Knowing.*
> *Sūratu 'l-Tawbah (The Repentance), 9:103*

That's one of the verses to purify you. It's a purification system. You cannot order people today, but this is an order. You cannot tell people today "give," as they feel you are interfering in their lives. But, Allāh ﷻ commanded, "*Yā Muhammad* ﷺ*, khudh min amwālihim ṣadaqatan.* Take from their money in donation."

Allāh ﷻ is saying very pointedly, "Don't leave it up to them or they won't give anything, its human character not to give. Don't ask, order them!"

---

[9] Sufism; the 15-century-old Islamic science "Purification of the Heart," comprised of specific spritiual practices to discipline the ego.

*Tuṭāhhirūḥ um wa tuzakkīhim bihā,* "you will clean them and you will purify them with it."

After Prophet ﷺ cleans you, you are purified. To distill waste water, first they clean it from contaminates, then they purify it. Allāh ﷻ is saying to Sayyīdīnā Muhammad ﷺ, "Don't wait for them to give voluntarily! Order them to give you from their money," *i.e.*, clean them. Your *ṣadaqah* prompts Prophet ﷺ to seek on your behalf, *"Yā Rabbī,* they helped me so help them," *i.e.*, the purification. Allāh ﷻ is saying to Sayyīdīnā Muhammad ﷺ, "When you take from them, you are obliged to give them something more than what they gave you (clean and purify them)."

*Wa ṣalli ʿalayhim,* "After you clean them and purify them, they become like angels."

That's why Prophet ﷺ said, *tuʿaradu ʿalayya ʿamal ummatī,* "I observe the deeds of my nation."

Prophet ﷺ continuously observes each person individually and simultaneously with no overlap. He is saying, "If I see good I thank Allāh ﷻ, and if I see bad I ask forgiveness on their behalf." Prophet ﷺ is constantly purifying his *Ummah.* But if you do more, Allāh ﷻ and His Prophet ﷺ will be obliged to grant you more. That's why when you present *awlīyāullāh* with a gift, they are obliged to give you a bigger gift. Don't say, "I am giving to the shaykh;" he is not in need and you are giving for yourself. Giving is not for the shaykh. When you give to him, he is now under obligation, as he will be asked on the Day of Judgment, "That person was generous and gave to you. What did you do for him?"

The *āyah* is clear: *tuṭāhhirūḥ um wa tuzakkīhim bihā,* "With their donation you have to clean them and purify them, then Allah ﷻ will be happy with you."

Allāh ﷻ went even further. "After you clean them, *wa ṣalli ʿalayhim,* send your *ṣalāt* on them, *yā* Muhammad."

When they give for a *masjid*, for a poor person, a charity, a guide, or a sincere person, then what about someone giving to Prophet ﷺ? What do you give to Prophet? We are his *Ummah*. *Ṣaḥābah* were giving directly, but we are far from that blessed time now, so what do we give? We give a charity, we give a mosque, we give to someone who is inheriting from Prophet ﷺ. There are many inheritors! Allāh ﷻ said in this *Ḥadīth Qudsī*:

> *My saints are under My domes and no one knows them except Me.* — *Imām Ghazālī, Hujwirī*

So that is a purification system that makes Prophet ﷺ send *ṣalawāt* on those who gave. *inna ṣalātaka sakanun lahum,* "Your *salāh* on them goes to your *Ummah,* and is peacefulness on them. Give them tranquility, peace, and happiness in their heart."

Don't expect that you will be helped if you are not showing generosity. Going through a *murshid* is not an easy way. He has power to clean you and he must show you he is cleaning you.

## The Murshid Observes and Tests His Followers

At university we had year-end exams. It was a big day for me and it came to my heart to visit Grandshaykh, may Allah bless his soul. It was 4 o'clock in the afternoon, and it is a three-hour drive from Beirut to Damascus. My brother and I wanted to go and pray 'Ishā with Grandshaykh ق and then return home by early morning, and the next day was the exam. I had already studied, but my mother was not happy. She loves Grandshaykh and Mawlana Shaykh, but she was not happy because when students have exams they must have discipline and prepare. We were young and we began to argue with her. "No, you must not go!", "yes, we will," "no", "yes", we like to go!" and she said, "Don't go!" Finally, I said, "I am going," and I took the car and we drove from Beirut to Damascus.

Look at the power of the *murshid*! Grandshaykh always stayed up in his private quarters. Before we knocked on his door and he opened it, saying, "Why you are coming here?" We could not say anything. He said, "Go back from where you came! Don't ever come to me when your mother is angry! Go, kiss her hand and ask forgiveness. If she gives permission, you can return. If not, don't come here!"

How he was able to see something that occurred hundreds of miles away? How did he know what we had done? It was a private discussion in our house, not public. Grandshaykh said some words which I am not going to repeat, and then sent us back. He was so filled with *jalāl* (magnificence and power) that we trembled in front of him. He did not allow us to step inside his home. So, we came back *alḥamdūlillāh*. Next day was the exam and I passed very well. My mother was happy. We said, "We want to go to Grandshaykh." She said, "Okay, no problem." So, we went there and Grandshaykh sent his helper to open the door. He said, "Mawlana wants to see you." Usually when you enter inside you must wait to see him. He said, "*Awlād* (children), come inside. I want to tell you something."

From the mercy they are sending on this gathering, I am saying, *awlīyāullāh* have permission from Prophet Muhammad ﷺ to look at their followers at least three times in every 24 hours, to see how they are behaving. If there is a problem, they have to fix it. Don't think the shaykh doesn't know anything. He does not necessarily tell you, and he appears as a normal person. But they know when you encounter things in your daily life, and they show you in ways that convince you that this is not just a lecture about *tasawwuf*.

Doctors study, and without training there is no permission to practice medicine. We must have a theory and practice, not just hearing the teachings but we must apply them through training, that's what is important.

Since last year, Mawlana Shaykh is under the *tajallī* (manifestation) of the Divine Name "aṣ-Ṣabūr". He likes to see his *murīds,* and his *murīds* like to see him. But, since he came under that Name, he is teaching his students patience. Are they going to be patient or not? Like today, some *murīds* are leaving when they have no chance to see Mawlana Shaykh. They were here for twelve days, and for sure in their heart their patience is exploding because they never spoke with Mawlana Shaykh or sat with him a little bit, and they came all the way here to Cyprus. So it was a test for them. Today I arrived here and saw people standing and no one was taking them up to meet Mawlana and I got them in. He was so happy to see them and he was so hospitable. From his side he likes to see everyone but he is also in seclusion.

About seclusion we say, *khalwatī, jalwatī,* "Complete seclusion sometimes with people, sometimes without people." Mawlana Shaykh is in that kind of situation today, being with people or not. He is under *ismullāh* aṣ-Ṣabūr, Allāh's Beautiful Name, "The Patient". It is the test for a *murīd* to see how much patience they have or don't have. *Taṣawwuf* is a training. How many people came, criticized, and left because they did not see the shaykh! Remember, it is a training here. You have to be patient! What is the benefit of *ṭarīqah* if you are going to have always candies and no tests?

When Grandshaykh ق called me and my brother into his room, he told us, "I observe you by the order of Prophet ﷺ at least three times every day. I see what you are doing, and by permission of Prophet ﷺ I send a tests on you and I send you problems. Don't expect I am going to give you candies, always sweet. Sweets you can have any time; go buy them from the grocery store. Am I going to tell you, 'Oh! You are the best, you are this, or you are that.' No, I am going to send you something to make you angry and test you. Are you angry or not? Are you patient or not? Because anger is the first bad characteristic that you must take away from yourself. I send on you three tests a day and you have to know when these come that I am watching, so don't misbehave! If you misbehave, you are losing your test at that time. Every time I send a test, you go higher. When you argued with your mother, I was the one talking through your mother. If you would have seen that, you would have been immediately raised higher in your levels."

I am now saying this to you out of mercy, so next time you will know. When you get angry, it means you are missing your opportunity to be raised up. Some people might ask, "Someone took our money and we got angry. Do we have a right to get our money back or do we leave it?" No, I am not saying to think like that, as to recover your money is your *dunyā* right. You can do whatever you want. I am saying, to get angry between brothers, sisters, parents, children, it is much better to be patient and calm; there is benefit in that.

For example, someone in this association criticizes you for brushing your teeth with toothpaste and toothbrush, saying it is *ḥarām*. They condemn you in such a way that you ask, "Did I do something wrong?" They answer, "Of course you did something wrong! You are following *kufr* now! Use the *miswāk*." Such people find many ways to upset their *murīd* brothers, saying things like, "You cannot clean your ears; you cannot blow your nose, it's *ḥarām* because that is from inside the body, so keep it inside," or, "don't go to the doctor, Allāh ﷻ will cure you."

These people are not *awlīyā*; they are normal people. If a *walī* says that, it is from wisdom. I saw Grandshaykh many times, wash his dentures with soap and other products before using them. The real issue is, first, those people are arguing, second, the shaykh might be testing if you will be patient with this brother who is bothering everyone. Those who say, "Never mind, *astaghfirullāh*," and they don't become angry, the shaykh is happy with them.

These are problems that confront you every day. You go to the market, you see an item is priced at ten dollars, you offer the seller five dollars and he curses you! Stay quiet; don't say anything, especially in Mecca and Madinah. They might tell you something costs fifty riyals, and you give them twenty riyals and they sell it to you! How it's fifty *riyals* and now it is twenty *riyals*? This is a business strategy. The trader operates based on a profit margin. But you cannot cheat the people who are coming there to take *barakah*.

In 1969, I was on Hajj with Mawlana Shaykh, may Allāh give him long life. Mawlana had with him fifty or sixty elderly *hajjis* (pilgrims) from Cyprus. I asked Mawlana why he brings these old people, when bringing younger people is easier. He brought men and women so old they cannot move well. Mawlana carried all their luggage, helped them on and off busses, something that is not easy when going through the desert. Today the bus route from Damascus to Madinah is 36 hours. In those days the trip was much longer, and busses broke down, the tire is gone, there is no air-conditioning, and you needed five or six days to reach. At every stop Mawlana had to help them off the bus. They slept in the desert or in the bus, and it was very difficult.

On this Hajj in 1969, he gave the passports to the *muṭawwif* (official) and there was someone who exchanges currency on the side. Mawlana went there, but the exchange rate we saw somewhere else was different than that person was giving us. Mawlana, me, and my brother were all wearing turban and *jubbah*. Mawlana said to the money exchanger, "The other one quoted me this price, and your price is so high." He looked at Mawlana and said, "You stupid shaykh, you (cursing)!" He exploded on Mawlana Shaykh, and Mawlana never opened his mouth. Then that person became even more angry because Mawlana didn't say anything. Such people want someone to reply so they can fight. Then that man spat on Mawlana! I was going to finish the situation, craziness came to my mind, but Mawlana Shaykh said, "No, keep patient." He did not let us do anything. Mawlana cleaned the spit off himself.

He went back to the building of the *muṭawwif* and someone sitting there asked Mawlana, "Shaykh, what do you need?"

Mawlana replied, "I am exchanging the money."

The person asked him, "How much are you exchanging?"

He was changing 1000 pounds for the *hajjis* to have a little to spend, but 1000 pounds was too much money at that time.

He said to Mawlana, "Okay, give me the one-thousand." He exchanged the pounds for riyals at an excellent exchange rate. Then at the end he added another 1000 pounds in the envelope and said, "This is from me to you, pray for me."

Mawlana Shaykh Nazim looked at us and said, "This is Grandshaykh. Allāh ﷻ sent that angry one to test us."

This is the power I am speaking about, the power of the *murshid*. The *murshid* has huge power, to observe what you are doing. This is similar to things about Murshid at-Tazkīyyah. We did not go above that. He has to be able to not be heedless for even one second from his *murīd*, his follower. He is with them all the time. Wherever they move, he is with them at least three times a day. Students of higher *murshids* will be under his observation 24 hours a day. So, may Allāh ﷻ give us from their teachings, not only learning, but training and practicing.

## Murshid at-Tazkiyyah Purifies His Followers

We have to train ourselves to be less angry, to hold our anger down, to be nice with people so they don't feel they did something wrong. But today they are angry and you are angry, and you cannot control the situation. Both of them are drunk. But, when he is drunk and you are patient, later he will notice that he harmed you and he will apologize. Some people don't apologize; never mind, you must not give your care to that, because you are doing for Allāh ﷻ.

Murshid -Tazkīyyah has to take away all your problems and purify you according the verse of Holy Qur'an that we mentioned previously, "Take from them donation by order." After all, there are many *murīds* who love the shaykh, to whom he can say , "Give this," and they will give.

When Mawlana gets support, he gives to people. Once someone came to Grandshaykh from the family of Prophet ﷺ. He had a very big problem, saying, "*Yā Sayyīdī*, I need two-thousand Syrian *lira* (equivalent of $500 US)." My brother and I were ready to give it, but we had to wait to see what Grandshaykh wanted. He said, "I don't like to ask anyone to give when he has doubt in his heart, or it becomes a problem on him. I don't want my *murīd* to be in a problem. So, those who have strong belief, I ask them. There are only two people with no doubt in their heart I can ask to give." He brought two and asked, "You give one-thousand, and you give one-thousand!" That was Mawlana Shaykh Nazim and his other *khalīfah*, Mawlana Shaykh Ḥusayn, and immediately they gave. We did not like that; we wanted to give, and Grandshaykh said, "No, not yet. For you now if I ask you to get something for me, I will pay for it. If you give voluntarily, I will accept it."

With *awlīyā* there are two ways: either they ask you to give or they leave it up to you to give voluntarily. If they tell you to give don't say "no", because they are trying to save you from a problem. But if they ask you get them a turban like yours because they like it, they have to give you the money for it. So what you give as a gift, they accept. But, if they ask you to get something for them, they will give you the money. And also they may ask you for something when they have no doubts about you; then they order you to give, as Allah ﷻ ordered Prophet ﷺ to take from the *Ṣaḥābah* to purify them. Three *Ṣaḥābah* committed a big mistake, and Prophet took from them one-third of their wealth to save them from the consequences of that mistake and to purify them.

When that verse of Holy Qur'an was revealed about the mistake of the three *Ṣaḥābah*, Prophet ﷺ did not say, "Give me two-and-a-half percent for *zakāt*." He took one-third of their total wealth to purify them. May Allāh ﷻ keep us under the Prophet ﷺ in his holy presence, at his door, and to be under *awlīyāullāh* always. And may Allāh ﷻ grant us to follow their ways, and may He remove any obstacles in their path wherever they are. *Amīn.*

## Surrender Like Sayyidina Ibrahim

Murshid at-Tazkīyyah has the power to send real visions and true dreams to his students wherever they are, and he delivers messages to them through dreams. It's not easy to reach *murīds* all around the world. That's why Allāh ﷻ ordered Prophet ﷺ and Prophet ordered *awlīyāullāh* to reach their followers through dreams.

Some people may say, "I have inspiration from my shaykh to do this or that." Sometimes inspiration is not clear, but a true dream is always clear. Inspiration may come with interference; you might be hallucinating and mistake that for inspiration. That's why we must be very careful. Some people say, "Mawlana Shaykh told me to do this." If you did not hear it from the tongue of Mawlana Shaykh, don't say, "Mawlana

Shaykh said this to me." There are many people who say, "I got an inspiration from the shaykh to do this." That is not correct. You may have seen something unclear, or from your imagination, or even from Shayṭān. But the true dream, *ru'yatu 'ṣ-ṣaliḥah,* is a real vision.

Like when the father of all prophets, Sayyīdinā Ibrāhīm ﷺ, said to his son, "Oh my son! I saw in the dream that I am slaughtering you." He was not arrogant.

Today some people think they reached a high level only if Mawlana Shaykh says to them, "Do *dhikr* here and there." They immediately assume they are connecting their hearts to shaykh and receiving information, then they begin to instruct *murīds* and appoint themselves as leaders. That's garbage! I'm sorry to say that. I am speaking to these cameras (for Sufilive.com live broadcast). Let them hear it. They are contaminating *murīds*!

Sayyīdīnā 'Ibrāhīm ﷺ said, "I saw in the dream," but you say you are seeing in a vision? In real life? How is that? Some even go so far as to claim, "I received from Rasūlullāh ﷺ." Go see their websites, where they claim to receive orders directly from Mawlana Shaykh Nazim, from Grandshaykh ق, and even from Rasūlullāh ﷺ! They don't say, "I saw in a dream." They get wrong information and say they are receiving directly from the shaykh.

We never heard Mawlana Shaykh Nazim say, "I receive directly," although he is the *sulṭān*, who must receive directly from Prophet ﷺ. But the doorkeeper cannot get directly; he must go through many other levels of spiritual development. There is too much sickness going around, unfortunately. About these issues people ask, "Why are you not taking it softly?"

These are very serious issues and you cannot be soft about them, petting and stroking people. In any other issue, no problem! You tell them, "You are good! You are a king! You are a lion! You are... whatever you want!" But in issues that undermine *ṭarīqah* you must be tough and address them quickly and firmly.

One very nice *murīd* sells small bottles of what he calls "holy water". When I asked about this, he said, "I have a farm with a water spring where we make *dhikr* of *Allāh Allāh, Allāh Allāh,* then fill these bottles with that holy water, which I call *rūḥ Mawlana,* 'Spirit of Mawlana'."

Three elements are at play here. I will elaborate on one, which is enough to make this point. Some people believe the water is as that *murīd* says and they buy it, so what you can say?

Sayyīdīnā 'Ibrāhīm ﷺ hid the knife and took his son, Sayyīdīnā Ismā'īl ﷺ, up on the mountain, intending to offer him as a sacrifice to Allāh ﷻ, just as *awlīyāullāh* give up their families and dedicate any personal, special life to their *murīds.*

He said, "Oh my son! We are going to play." The *sīrah* (biography) states Sayyīdīnā Ismāīl ﷺ was around nine years old.

His father told him, "Let's play 'hide and seek'. I will close your eyes and you find me."

Sayyīdīnā Ismāīl ﷺ answered, "O my father! Do whatever you have been ordered! Don't delay!"

Sayyīdīnā 'Ibrāhīm ﷺ put the knife to slaughter his son, but Allāh ﷻ ordered the knife not to cut. Again Sayyīdīnā 'Ibrāhīm ﷺ tried with all his energy to cut the neck of his son!

*Ṭarīqah* is not easy. If you don't step on your ego and kill your ego with Sayyīdīnā Ibrahim's ﷺ knife, you will not see what cannot be seen, or hear what cannot be heard, or speak what people cannot speak. In the famous *Ḥadīth* Qudsi about *iḥsān* (Station of Perfection), Prophet ﷺ states:

*(Allah said) "As long as My servant approaches me through voluntary worship, I will love him. If I love him, I will be his eyes through which he sees, I will be his ears with which he hears, I will be his tongue with which he speaks, I will be his hand with which he senses, and I will be the legs with which he walks."*

Sayyīdīnā ʿIbrāhīm ﷺ tried another time to fulfill the holy command and that was burning his heart from inside. Sayyīdīnā Ismāʿīl ﷺ said, "O my father! What kind of barbeque are you making?"

He answered, "O my son! My heart is burning for your light, for your love."

This is a prophet who gave his son to Allāh ﷻ as a sacrifice. Do you think *awlīyāullāh* are not inheriting that, to give up their lives and their desires? *Awlīyāullāh* gave their lives for their followers, and what did they get in return? Of course they got happiness and satisfaction from Allāh ﷻ and His prophets, but their life is devoted to carrying everyone's sins and mistakes. How many people come to the shaykh's presence, which is a Divinely Presence, with all their dirtiness and bad gossips in their hearts and minds?

So Sayyīdīnā ʿIbrāhīm ﷺ tried seventy times but the knife did not cut. In frustration, he shouted at the knife, "I am following Allāh's order! O knife, why aren't you cutting?! Why are you delaying Allāh's order?" And the knife answered, "Why are you criticizing me? I am also carrying out Allāh's order! Why didn't you complain on the fire of Nimrod when it didn't burn you?! Because it was Allāh's order to the fire not to burn you, *yā* ʿIbrāhīm, and Allāh ordered me not to cut the neck of your son."

He fulfilled Allah's order, Allah ﷻ accepted that, then Sayyīdinā Ibrāhīm ﷺ was able to move through that test. The sacrifice of his son was symbolizedby sacrificing a huge ram.

*wa nādaynāhu an yā Ibrāhīm. qad ṣadaqta ar-ru'yā innā kadhālika najzī 'l-muḥsinīn.*

*And We called out to him, "O Abraham! You have fulfilled the vision!" Verily! Thus do We reward the doers of good.*

*Sūratu 'ṣ-Ṣāffāt (Those Arrayed in Ranks), 37:105*

*Ru'yā* is a vision. First in the *āyah* it was described as a dream, and when he passed that test Allāh ﷻ opened the vision. This is a lesson for us, that if you move in Allāh's Way, be humble enough to say, "It is a dream," instead of saying, "My shaykh is telling me to tell my *murīds* this." Some self-appointed ones have ten or fifteen *murīds*. They order them to do this and do that, as if an order is coming from the shaykh in a vision. Because of Sayyīdinā Ibrāhīm's humbleness, Allah ﷻ changed his dream to a vision.

*Irshād* is not something easy; you have to pass from the dreams to visions. Who can see Mawlana Shaykh in reality? Who can see Prophet ﷺ in reality? Don't lie, because when the *Ṣaḥābah* asked Prophet ﷺ, "Does a *mu'min* lie?" Prophet ﷺ answered, "A *mu'min* never lies!" We lie to each other, but we cannot lie to Allāh ﷻ. We are lying to Allāh ﷻ by not fulfilling promises we made on the Day of Promises. That is very important.

Mawlana Shaykh said on the Day of Promises, Allāh took a promise from every one, of what he has to do in *dunyā*. Every one of us! When He asked us, *alastu bi rabbikum,* "Am I not your Lord?" we answered, "Yes!" At that time, Allāh ﷻ took from every one a promise, "You have to do this, and this, and this, and this, and this." When you don't do it, you are lying and breaking your promise.

Did you sign a contract with Allāh ﷻ? Definitely! Today when you buy a house, they give you long contract, many pages in small print, instructing you to, "Sign here, and here, and here." Do you read those hundred pages of the contract? You cannot! You give it to a lawyer. Even if a comma is not in its place, the agreement takes on a completely different meaning. So, that lawyer's specialty is contracts. If you don't give it to a lawyer, it could be at any moment you breach that contract. If you make one mistake, the whole contract is null, finished, and you are penalized: you lose something.

So in Allāh's Presence when we said, "*Yā Rabbī*! *Ash-hādu an lā ilāha illa-Llāh, wa ash-hādu anna Muḥammadan ʿabduhu wa rasūluh,*" it was an honor for us to be Muslim. We signed a contract stipulating, "You are our Lord, and Muhammad ﷺ is Your messenger." We signed that contract and it is binding. It's not one-hundred pages: every breath we take is tied to that contract! How many breaths do you have? Do you know? Every moment of your life is a breath coming in or going out. So don't count your life by years; heavenly counting is by how many breaths Allāh ﷻ gave to you and that is your age. In every breath there is a meaning, a secret. You agreed to it on the Day of Promises.

That's why you need that lawyer—the *murshid* is your lawyer. *MashāAllāh,* no one here is appointing himself as a shaykh, to make *dhikr* and lectures, going back to his country with full *ijāzah* from his ego, becoming like a huge beast, like lion he cannot control! It's better to be a sheep; you can graze anywhere and easily find food. Some become lions because they want to eat human beings. That's why those who think they are authorized on *irshād* have the characters of lions. I'm not speaking on *dhikr*; anyone can do *dhikr*, even a 10-year-old child can lead *dhikr*. What is the issue? Those false ones who believe they are guides and who give imaginary guidance are lions, eating the flesh of their *murīds*.

So we need a lawyer to read our contract. Did Mawlana read your contract? You don't know. For sure, yes. He is not waiting for you to do what is written there. He is going to do that on your behalf. That's the importance. He's not waiting for you, not waiting for me, not waiting for anyone, because he knows you cannot do it! He will do it on our behalf. Mawlana has the power of *aṭ-ṭayy*:

> *That Day, We will fold up Heaven like folding the pages of a book.* *Sūratu 'l-Anbīyā (The Prophets), 21:104*

Like folding clothes, and today better than that, today we can put our clothes in "space bags" and vacuum out all the air, compacting that mass into a fraction of the space. *Awlīyāullāh* have *ṭayy al-lisān*, the power to fold their tongue, which allows their recitation of *dhikrullāh*, to be at rocket speed, so they read everything easily, quickly.

That's why when he was ordered for *irshād*, Grandshaykh 'AbdAllāh al-Fā'iz ad-Dāghestānī said to his teacher, Shaykh Sharafuddīn, "*Yā Sayyīdī*, I have one condition to accept *irshād*, if it is to work. If my condition is granted, I accept." Today if Mawlana will say to someone, "I am giving you *irshād*," he will not refuse it, saying, "I don't want, except on a condition." That one will run to get anything, a piece of paper even, and he would make a stamp with Mawlana's name and stamp that paper, to make it official! You can write whatever you like, stamp it, and show everyone that you have *ijāzah*![10]

How do they claim livestock? They stamp (brand) them. So these people are stamped already. Mawlana knows they are using their stamp and he stamps them.

When Grandshaykh was selected to receive *irshād*, he said, "No, I don't want it; leave it. Why should I want it? Why take that burden? I am happy secluding myself. I am making *dhikrullāh* in the holy presence of *awlīyāullāh*, in the holy presence of Prophet ﷺ, and in the Divine Presence of Allāh ﷻ. I am happy! Why should I be responsible for all these people?

---

[10] Permission, authorization; in this case, permission from one's shaykh to lead, to represent, to teach, etc.

That one who is mentally disturbed, another who has a sickness in his heart, that one with bad manners."

Here in the *dargah*, I saw someone come from the window where Mawlana was sitting for Jumuʿah and push him, saying, "Shaykh, Shaykh! Shaykh, Shaykh!" He gave some cloves to Mawlana and, out of humbleness, Mawlana didn't say anything: he read on them and gave them back to that rude one. That aggressive one said, "No, Shaykh, Shaykh!" again pushing Mawlana, crazy that Mawlana was not looking at him. He pushed Mawlana again, saying, "No! I brought these for you! This is *barakah* from me to you!" Mawlana humbly put that in his pocket, so calmly, so softly, although that person was so aggressive.

So Grandshaykh said, why be humiliated? Sit by yourself and enjoy a peaceful life. Be a sheep, don't be a shepherd. Don't be a guide, you don't need that! Those people who are running to be shaykhs, take it! Be happy! We will be sheep, *alḥamdūlillāh*, with no need to carry that responsibility.

Grandshaykh answered, "Ask Prophet ﷺ, if he will excuse me from it, then I am happy." The next day in the association of *awlīyāullāh* with Prophet ﷺ, through real visions Shaykh Sharafuddīn presented that reply, and Prophet ﷺ said, "Ask him why, and what he wants." Why, Prophet doesn't know? He knows. Shaykh Sharafuddīn doesn't know? He knows. This event is for us to learn.

As instructed, Shaykh Sharafuddīn asked Grandshaykh, who answered, *"Yā Sayyīdī*, when Prophet went into *miʿrāj* Allāh ordered him to make fifty prayers daily. He kept reducing it by Prophet ﷺ asking, '*Yā Rabbī*! Reduce it, reduce it.' Sayyīdīnā Mūsā advised him, 'I tried that with my people, but they are lazy and they are not going to pray. So your *Ummah* is also not going to pray. Ask Allāh ﷻ to reduce it.' Prophet ﷺ asked Allāh ﷻ until it came to five prayers daily. *Yā*

*Sayyīdī*! I know our *murīds* are lazy. One day they do *awrād*, one day they won't. Even if they do it every day, sometimes their hearts are not with Allāh and His Prophet. They might do some sins. So I don't want to look at what they are doing, good or not. I am asking that if I give them initiation and they sit in my presence even for five minutes, let me raise them to my level of knowledge, and in the Day of Judgment they will be in Paradise. If this condition is accepted, I will take *irshād*. I am not going to wait for anyone to achieve anything."

That is why Mawlana doesn't say to anyone, "Do this or that," because he is taking their burden and completing their obligations on their behalf!

So Shaykh Sharafuddīn, next day went to Prophet ﷺ in that vision and he said, "*Yā Rasūlullāh,* this is his answer." Prophet ﷺ said, "I am happy with that answer, because no one ever asked for that!" So may Allāh ﷻ keep us on the way of *awlīyāullāh*.

In his notes, Grandshaykh ق said Murshid at-Tazkīyyah is aware of his breath; not one breath is inhaled or exhaled with heedlessness. He is always in the presence of Prophet ﷺ. With every breath, he has to use his tongue with *ṭayyu 'l-lisān,* folding time and space, to recite a minimum of 700,000 times *dhikrullāh* in one breath. And this is only the second level of *irshād,* not the third or fourth level!

Can any student around the world ordered to do *dhikr* claim they have that power? We are watching TV and reciting "Allāh, Allāh, Allāh, Allāh, Allāh, Allāh, Allāh." Or you are watching what your wife or your children are doing, while you recite *dhikr*. It means your heart is not present. The heart of the *murshid* is always present. They do not grant that station without giving you that high level of *dhikrullāh*.

## Sultan adh-Dhikr

According to Grandshaykh's notes, the last characteristic of Murshid at-Tazkīyyah is that he has to complete 100,000 *dhikrullāh* in a moment or in one hour. Not like us; it takes us half-an-hour to make 5,000 *dhikrullāh,* or some people take one hour, others may take ten minutes depending on how fast they are. But *awlīyāullāh* can recite up to 700,000 in a moment or in less than one hour. How are the tongue and heart able to recite so quickly, 700,000 by tongue and by heart Allāh knows how much? There is no comparison between the heart and the tongue. The tongue can do 700,000 in a moment, and the heart can do an infinite number, depending on the power of that *walī*; he may be able to recite seven million or 70 million, Allāh knows!

The answer is, under the tongue there is a spiritual vein that goes directly to the heart, since when we were in the womb of our mother. When we began breastfeeding and later eating food, we entered a negative, polluted environment that slowly placed darkness veils on that vein, until eventually it became completely dark. When we became disciples of a shaykh, that darkness already existed. When the shaykh asks you to make an *awrād*, you may feel sleepy and begin to yawn. Why? There is a purification Shayṭān doesn't want to occur, so he distracts you with sleep. With *dhikrullāh* that veil is going to disappear, veil after veil, so sleepiness, yawning and gossips of the mind come quickly, because you are reducing the darkness veils and Shayṭān is not happy. If you continue your *awrād*—even with laziness, but making sure you finish it—slowly, slowly, the darkness will become an enlightened connection. Light will fill that place and you will be able to see it going from the tongue to the heart.

Light moves 300,000 kilometers per second. How? If you want to physically move 300,000 kilometers, how long will it take? But with the speed of light, you can move with no problem. The speed of the light between your tongue and your heart will move at least 300,000 kilometers per second! That's why at the very lowest level, *awlīyāullāh* move at that speed. They move in space through spiritual power and they can move their tongue through that power. That's why they can reach even up to 70 million *dhikrullāh* per second. If you want to divide 300,000 kilometers per second, how long will it take you to move your foot forward? Would it take one second? So what about the tongue? Physicists studied what is the smallest fraction of time we can count, and they measured nanoseconds, microseconds or milliseconds, until they found a measurement through which time itself disappears! Then what will appear? Energy; time is gone and only energy remains. There is no past, present, or future, only energy. That's why *awlīyāullāh* don't relate to time, because they are in an energy-based environment. They move in energy and energy never disappears: it is always there. So whenever they move, they move with energy, where time and distance from the physical world do not exist. That's how they move in space and reach their followers.

When *awlīyāullāh* do *dhikr* in such a way, it is known as "Sulṭān adh-Dhikr": *dhikr* of the tongue that has control over time because it moves with energy, as we say in Arabic:

> *Fa idhā dhahabat ʿayni'ẓ-ẓulmata wa ṣāra nūr inayā yaṭīq ʿalā dhālika bilā kharq li 'l-ʿaqal.*
> *If the source of darkness has gone from him, he will become enlightened, able to withstand that without going beyond his mind.*

When those veils of darkness are lifted, the tongue becomes illuminated with that spiritual power and can move in massive speeds wherever it likes. Their heart and every cell of their body is saying *Allāh, Allāh, Allāh, Allāh.* It is estimated there are three trillion cells in the human body, rejuvenated every six months; old cells are replaced by new cells. Bodies and entire systems of *awlīyāullāh* are praising Allāh ﷻ! Imagine if every cell is saying *Allāh, Allāh,* in one second they say *dhikrullāh* three trillion times. How can we understand this? That's why *taṣawwuf* is not easy to understand. You can hear lectures on *tasawwuf,* but without giving it a basic structure people cannot understand. What's the benefit of speaking about *ma'arifatullah* when you don't have a base? This will give us a base. That's how powerful *awlīyāullāh* are.

And Allāh rewards our *'amal* ten times more, so three trillion becomes 30 trillion! And according to the *Ḥadīth* Qudsi of Prophet, Allāh ﷻ said:

*If someone remembers Me, I remember him in a better Presence than his presence.*

O Muslims! There are many secrets within spirituality and I will touch on one of them. What is Sulṭān adh-Dhikr? Grandshaykh asked and answered this question at the same time. He said nine of the *awlīyā* of the Naqshbandi Golden Chain have the power of Sulṭān adh-Dhikr.

*'innā naḥnu nazzalnā adh-dhikra wa 'innā lahu laḥāfiẓ.*
*It is We Who have sent down the dhikr (Holy Qur'an) and surely, We will guard it (from corruption).*
*Sūratu 'l-Ḥijr (The Rocky Tracks), 15:9*

"We revealed the Holy Qur'an, We are protecting it from any addition or subtraction, and We are protecting it from any enemy until the Day of Judgment. It's our holy revelation to Sayyīdina Muhammad ﷺ."

So when you read Holy Qur'an from beginning to end, you say you completed recitation of Holy Qur'an on every letter— *alif, lām, mīm, kāf* —and no matter how often any letter is repeated, each time you recite it, it has a different spiritual manifestation and meaning. *Awlīyāullāh* receive a minimum of 12,000 different manifestations of oceans of *maʿrifatullāh*[11] on every letter they recite! Prophet ﷺ reveals to their hearts up to 24,000 knowledges of *maʿrifatullāh* on every letter of Holy Qur'an. So what will you say about *maʿrifatullāh*?

In his seclusion now, Mawlana Shaykh Nazim enters into 12,000 to 24,000 oceans of knowledges for every letter of Holy Qur'an he recites. So their recitation of Holy Qur'an is different from ours. *Awlīyāullāh* complete Holy Qur'an in this way: when they read it once from beginning to end, on every letter they are receiving 12,000 to 24,000 knowledges from oceans of *maʿrifatullāh*. Another time they read it and another knowledge comes, another time they read it, different oceans come; that is the normal level for *awlīyāullāh*. But recitation of Sulṭān adh-Dhikr is different. Sayyīdīna Abū Yazīd al-Bistāmi ق was able to read it once (as mentioned in the book, *The Naqshbandi Sufi Way*). Whatever *awlīyāullāh* reach through oceans of *maʿrifatullāh* all accumulated together, he was able to read it once in his life and get that power!

If every *walī* reads from the beginning to the end of his life, from 12,000 up to 24,000 oceans of knowledge appear on every letter he reads. If he reads the Holy Qur'an a thousand times, multiply that by 12,000 to 24,000 knowledges he received on every letter, then add what the 7007 *awlīyāullāh* of the Naqshbandi Sufi Order received! Once in his life, Sayyīdīna Abū Yazīd al-Bistāmi ق was able to read the Holy Qur'an as if all *awlīyā* are getting all these manifestations. Some *awlīyā* read Sulṭān adh-Dhikr three times, others six times or more.

---

11 Gnosis; heavenly knowledge pertaining to Allāh.

Grandshaykh, may Allāh bless him, said, "My shaykh[12], Shaykh Sharafuddīn, has a special way of reciting the Holy Qur'an with the power of Sulṭān adh-Dhikr on every breath (Ṭayyu 'l-Lisān). With every inhalation he completed Holy Qur'an, and with every exhalation he completed Holy Qur'an with the secret of Sulṭān adh-Dhikr, and still the Holy Qur'an has many never-ending secrets, and one is not the same as the other."

Allah is al-'Aẓīm! Whatever you say about the Holy Qur'an, Allāh ﷻ is above it. Shaykh Sharafuddīn and Grandshaykh 'AbdAllāh and Mawlana Shaykh Nazim have no permission to say they achieved that. Imagine someone in every breath, every three-to-four seconds, completes the Holy Qur'an and accumulating 12,000 to 24,000 oceans of knowledge for every letter! That demonstrates Allāh's love toward *awlīyā*. We are very honored to be connected to Mawlana Shaykh Nazim!

Grandshaykh, may Allāh bless his soul, said that for every 1,000 *awlīyāullāh,* only two wives acknowledge him as a *walī*. Only two out of 1,000 might know the importance of their husbands; the rest know nothing and are not concerned.

The *maqām* of Sayyīdina Jamaluddin al-Ghumuqi al-Ḥusayni, may Allāh bless his soul, is in Uskudar, in Istanbul; whoever visits his *maqām,* Allāh will give him two eyes in *Ākhirah,* one above his belly and one under his belly. So when you visit Istanbul, go there—he is ready for you, most welcome.

Once Sayyīdina Jamaluddīn al-Ghumūqī al-Ḥusaynī ق was preparing to go to Jumu'ah. He dressed in his best dress and combed his beard. He had two special eyes; one above his

---

[12] Grandshaykh ق did not speak about himself; he hides it, but when he speaks about his shaykh, it means he has reached that level.

belly and one under his belly. The one above his belly saw through heavens up to Sidratu 'l-Muntahā. The one under his belly saw through the seven earths. Allāh gave him that power, and yet his wife did not see his value.

He was observing Allāh's order to wear your best ornaments (physical and spiritual) and go to any mosque. You don't only go to the *masjid* dressed in your best attire when your heart is dirty; take it with purity, Allāh ﷻ likes that. So according to the *sunnah* of Prophet ﷺ and verses of the Holy Qur'an, *awlīyāullāh* wear their best clothes to Jumuʿah.

His wife asked him angrily, "Where are you going?" He didn't answer. She wanted to argue and make trouble for him. Sayyīdinā Jamaluddīn ق left the house to walk to the *masjid*. His wife was doing laundry and as soon as he passed under the window, she threw the dirty laundry water on his head! He didn't open his mouth; he is *musallim,* submitted to Allah ﷻ, like Mawlana Shaykh Nazim ق submits to everything.

When will those who make themselves controllers at the door be kicked out? They decide, "This one can come out and this one cannot come out." They are spiritual racists! Their faces are yellow like Yājūj and Mājūj. They don't believe in Allāh ﷻ; they are secularists. If you kick them out, they come from the window like *jinn*. They want to control everything. We say, *Inna Allāha yumhil wa lā yuḥmil*. It means Allāh ﷻ gives wrongdoers a chance, but He does not ignore what they do; will they repent, or not? If not now, one day He will punish you.

*Awlīyāullāh* are in an ocean of submission. She poured that dirty water on his head to prevent him from going to Jumuʿah. That was a wife of a *walī* of the Naqshbandi Golden Chain. Allāh is testing; don't think He is not testing his *awlīyā*. As much as they grow closer there are bigger tests, even in the privacy of their homes. So be happy that we are not being tested, because we don't have the position to take people up or down, as that is a big test. Let us be sheep!

So how did the shaykh react? He went quickly to one of his *murīds*, took clean clothes from him, showered, dressed, prayed Ṣalātu 'l-Jumu'ah at the mosque and returned home. She expected him to fight with her but he was smiling as if nothing happened.

If you were faced with that situation, what would you do? At a minimum you would scold her! But he did not open his mouth; he knew if he did, he would be losing. He didn't say anything and Allāh ﷻ rewarded him.

Once when Prophet ﷺ prepared to go to the *masjid*, he combed his hair and Sayyida 'Āyesha ؓ asked, "*Yā Rasūlullāh*! Where are you going?" In other words, "Are you getting married to another one?"

She became jealous, and she is from Ummahātu 'l-Mu'minīn, Mothers of the Believers! Ladies have that in their hearts; Allāh created that, which is good for many things.

Prophet ﷺ replied, "O 'Āyesha!! A believer is the mirror of his brother," which means, "What you are seeing is the mirror of your own character."

Mawlana Shaykh Nazim, may Allāh give him long life, is our mirror for us to observe their behavior and learn; see what kind of difficulties they are carrying and still they are smiling. They are like that. So that's why Allāh granted the power to read Sulṭān adh-Dhikr to those few *awlīyāullāh* and not to all. They are inheritors of Prophet Muhammad ﷺ. May Allāh ﷻ keep us in their ways!

Sometimes people don't like what we are saying and they try to block the ladies from entering Mawlana Shaykh's house because they are controlling them. People are fed up from that and they don't like those who are creating difficulties for everyone to visit Mawlana Shaykh. Those troublemakers want Mawlana only to see what they like, but a day will come when *Allāhu yumhil wa lā yuhmil,* and they will disappear!

May Allāh ﷻ forgive us.

*Wa min Allāhi 't-tawfīq, bi ḥurmati 'l-ḥabīb, bi ḥurmati 'l-Fātiḥah.*
*And with Allāh is success. For the sake of the Beloved, for his sake we recite the opening chapter of Holy Qur'an.*

# Murshid at-Tasfiyyah: Guide of Sifting

*Madad yā Sulṭān al-Awlīyā, Shaykh Muḥammad Nāẓim al-Ḥaqqānī.*
*Madad yā Sulṭān al-Awlīyā, Shaykh ʿAbdAllāh al-Fā'iz ad-Dāghestānī.*

We are ordered to obey those on authority, which are of two types: first, the rulers of countries, whose laws we must obey; and second, the rulers of spiritualities, rulers of hearts, whom we must listen to and obey as they will guide us to where we need to go.

*Atīʿūllāha wa atʿīū 'r-Rasūla wa ūli 'l-amri minkum.*
*Obey Allāh, obey Prophet ﷺ, and obey those who are on authority.* *Sūratu 'n-Nisā (The Women), 4:59*

After Murshid at-Tazkīyyah tried his best to train the people, to purify their hearts from the temptations of Shayṭān and the sickness of their egos, he raises them up to his level. Now, because his level is limited also, he takes them to the presence of Murshid at-Taṣfīyyah, the Guide of Sifting. When you mine gold, it is mixed with dirt, so you wash it to sift the gold from the dirt. You get the cream of the community, the cream of the students, the cream of those who are the best in the eyes of the guide. You will not lose what you have been trained with and what you have learned from the Guide of Purification; no, you are now in their level. But some people can pass for higher education in very complex studies.

Murshid at-Taṣfīyyah chooses the best of the community, the best of the students, who he begins to train to reach his level. We are speaking now about his characteristics, according to Grandshaykh's and Mawlana Shaykh Nazim's explanations, which I am quoting.

## Characteristics of Murshid at-Tasfiyyah

Murshid at-Taṣfīyyah, the third level of *irshād*, must have the characteristics of Murshid at-Tabarruk and Murshid at-Tazkīyyah. Grandshaykh ق is saying, characteristics of all guides that have attained the two first levels will be reflected on Murshid at-Taṣfīyyah. There is not only one guide in the first level, there are many. Many *awlīyā* carry the first level, the second level and the third level, but the fourth level, the top of the pyramid, is only with the Sulṭān al-Awlīyā. The current Sulṭān al-Awlīyā is Mawlana Shaykh Muhammad Nazim al-Haqqani, may Allāh bless him, bless his powers and bless us for his sake! *Amīn.*

The first characteristic of Murshid at-Taṣfīyyah, the one who carries the elite students, is that he is *zāhid* (ascetic) from everything. He is no longer a slave to *dunyā; dunyā* becomes his slave and runs after him.

As Prophet ﷺ mentioned in his *ḥadīth*, and Grandshaykh ق mentioned, that once at Ishrāq time Prophet ﷺ called his *Ṣaḥābah,* who were training at Uḥud in the early morning while it was still cool outside. Prophet ﷺ stood facing the mountain. The sun was rising and he lined up the *Ṣaḥābah* and said to them, "Look at the mountain of Uḥud." They gave their back to Prophet ﷺ because they are looking to the mountain. When they stood up in a line looking at the mountain, the sun was behind them, so immediately their shadows were in front of them. Prophet ﷺ said, "I want you to run! Whoever can catch his shadow, I will give him my *jubbah.*"

*Ṣaḥābah* never used their minds in the presence of Prophet ﷺ. Also, you cannot use your mind in the presence of *awlīyāullāh,* who are inheritors of Prophet Muhammad ﷺ and of other prophets: you have to accept. You come to them seeking guidance, they answer you, then you take what they give. If you don't want to do what they say, then do what you know and don't ask them for guidance, because whenever you question the order, more difficulty will come in the answer. For example, Allāh ﷻ ordered Sayyīdīnā Mūsā ﷺ and the Bani Israel to slaughter a cow. They did not want to pay for a cow, so they began to ask questions, such as what kind of eyes does it have, what color is it, what size. With each question, Allāh ﷻ gave a further description, which also made it extremely rare. So it became so difficult to find a cow that fit that particular description, and when they did it was so expensive!

You must know that sometimes Mawlana may answer you the opposite of what you like, so be careful what you ask for and how you react to the answer. Once the *Ṣaḥābah* asked Prophet ﷺ, "It's time to graft the trees. Can we graft the palm trees?" He answered, "Yes, this year will be the best." They grafted those palm trees, all of which died! They asked, "*Yā Rasūlullāh*, we did what you said, but the trees died." He ﷺ said, "I came to complete your *Ākhirah*, not your *dunyā*. Ask who knows about *dunyā*."

So when Prophet ﷺ instructed the *Ṣaḥābah*, "Run after your shadow; if you catch it, I will give you my robe," they didn't ask why, because it is impossible to catch one's shadow. They ran after it, but of course the shadow was also running, until they reached the mountain. Then Prophet ﷺ said to them, "Look at me and run to me." They ran to him and their shadows were behind them, because the sun was in the east (behind them), and they ran west. Prophet ﷺ said, "When you are running after *dunyā* it makes you a slave to her and you cannot catch it. But when you run to me, toward your *Ākhirah*, your *dunyā* will run behind you like the shadow is now running behind you. I am coming for *Ākhirah*, not *dunyā*."

When we say someone is *zāhid*, immediately it comes to our mind that he is *zāhid* of *dunyā*. Grandshaykh said, "Murshid at-Tazkīyyah must be *zāhid* from *Ākhirah*. He doesn't want anything from *Ākhirah,* he wants only the Divine Presence of his Lord, Almighty Allāh ﷻ."

Sayyīdīnā Abū Yazīd al-Bistāmi said, "*Yā Rabbī,* make my body as big as Hell. I don't mind; I'm not afraid of your Hellfire. I want to save the whole *Ummah,* because I love You, and they are Your Creation. Make my body as big as Hell, so that no one will enter except me and everyone will be safe." This is an example of being *zāhid* in *Ākhirah.* Who else can claim that?

Prophet ﷺ asked, "*Yā* Abū Hurayrah, when you read the verse of Holy Qur'an:

> *Those who remember Allāh (and mention His Beautiful Names and Attributes) while standing, sitting, and lying down on their sides, and think deeply about the creation of the heavens and the Earth, (saying): "Our Lord! You have not created (all) this without purpose, Glory to You! Give us salvation from the torment of the Fire.*
>
> *Sūrat Ālī-'Imrān (The Family of Imrān), 3:191*

"Standing" means when you are awake, going, coming, walking, moving, whatever, your heart is busy. "When you are sitting" means when you are at home with your family still your heart is with Allāh ﷻ. "When you are lying down" means when you are sleeping. It means when you reach the level that in 24 hours you remain occupied with remembrance of Allāh ﷻ. *Ṣaḥābah* reached that level.

People think the creation of a human being is more complex than the creation of the universe. Scientists conclude that when the Big Bang occurred, the universe already existed. Allāh ﷻ said:

> *The Creation of heavens and Earth is more difficult than creation of human beings." Sūratu 'l-Ghāfir (The Clement), 40:57*

But, many people don't know He said at the end of this *āyah, wa lākinna akthara an-nāsi lā yaʿlamūn,* "But most of Mankind know not."

In our galaxy, in every moment our sun generates energy at 50 million degrees centigrade, equivalent to an atomic reaction. Imagine what fuel it is generating from years and years—Allāh knows how many years the sun existed—and it never finished, still shooting these atomic reactions, more than hydrogen bombs and explosions. Who is doing it? What kind of fire makes that intense heat?

So, Prophet ﷺ said, "*Yā* Abū Hurayrah, what do you think about that, your reflection on Earth?"

He answered, "*Yā Rasūlullāh*! When I reflect, I see the universe indicates the greatness of Allāh ﷻ!"

Prophet ﷺ said, "*Yā*, Abū Hurayrah, if you contemplate in such a way for one hour a day, you will be rewarded as if you worshipped one entire day." So, meditation is important. Allāh knows best what you learn when meditating to statues, pictures, candles, or on this and that. That is an imitation of real meditation which, to understand, you must examine the most important point, what Allāh is mentioning in Holy Qur'an.

Then he saw Sayyīdinā Ibn ʿAbbās ؓ, and Prophet ﷺ said, "*Yā* Ibn ʿAbbās, what about this verse of Holy Qur'an? What do you contemplate when you read that āyat?"

He answered, "*Yā Sayyīdī, Yā Rasūlullāh.* When I think about that, I am seeing the greatness of how Allah ﷻ created every star in space, how every constellation is static, how the moon orbits the Earth, how the Earth's spinning create day and night and its prolonged orbit creates months, and how orbits of the sun and moon creates years. And I am wondering where you will send me here and there, in this huge universe we are in."

To summarize, Prophet ﷺ answered, "*Yā* Ibn ʿAbbās, for that contemplation, you will be rewarded as if you worshipped one year."

For one hour of contemplation on Allāh's greatness, on His creation of this universe and your being, Allāh ﷻ will give you the reward of one year of real worship, because our worship is like imitation worship. When we say *Allāhu Akbar* to begin our prayer, how many thoughts come, how many whisperings from Shayṭān or other distractions? So, when Prophet ﷺ says you will be rewarded with "one year of worship," it means it is a pure worship without any sin mixed in it. That's why we should reflect daily even for five minutes. You don't need to get one year's reward—get one week or one day for contemplating for one minute! Close your eyes, connect with your shaykh, and from Mawlana Shaykh to Prophet ﷺ for one minute—it is enough to begin.

Then Prophet ﷺ passed by Sayyīdīnā Abū Bakr aṣ-Ṣiddīq ق and said, "*Yā* Abū Bakr, what about this verse of Holy Qur'an?" And he said, "*Yā Sayyīdī, Yā Rasūlullāh,* I think about that verse and I see your *Ummah,* and I see a human being. I say, '*Yā Rabbī,* let the heat of *lahāb* (the intense heat from the fire of Hell) to come on me alone and the whole *Ummah* will be saved.'" Prophet ﷺ said, "*Yā* Abū Bakr, The way you reflect your thought, you will be rewarded more than the worship of seventy years."

It means when you say, *Yā Rabbī,* for the love of Sayyīdīnā Muhammad ﷺ, I am giving up my *dunyā* and my *Ākhirah* and do whatever You want. I want to be like Your Earth, that people can step on me."

Mawlana Shaykh is in seclusion. When he meets with people, for sure they carry the pollution of this *dunyā,* mingling with all kind of lifestyles and people. That negative energy is reflected immediately on Mawlana Shaykh. That's why it's not easy for someone to carry that responsibility unless he is inheriting directly from Prophet ﷺ and especially through the line of Sayyīdīnā Abū Bakr Siddiq ق. These *awlīyā* are giving their lives for the *Ummah*. If they see you or they don't see you, it's no problem. As soon as you make your intention, step out from your home with the intention to visit, from that moment he is carrying you and all your problems, besides carrying you as a student!

Murshid at-Taṣfīyyah is the one that can choose the elite of the *murīds*. He has to be *zāhid* of *Ākhirah*. He is under an obligation that sometimes Mawlana says, "Do this," but he doesn't insist on it. You do it or not do it, it's up to you. No, it's an obligation because you are already in that journey of guidance. He passed the two levels before him, *tabarruk* and *tazkiyyah*, and now comes to *tasfiyyah*, and he knows he must carry that obligation coming from his real *murshid*.

Sometimes people think their real *murshid* is this man, but no, he is an imitational *murshid*, and he has nothing to give them. It's not easy to be a *murshid*. You can be someone who gives a presentation, a seminar, a conference, a speech; it's okay, no problem, but guidance is completely different. To impart guidance, he must know where you are and raise you up to his level; also, he must take from you your problems every 24 hours. Every moment in your life they are able to see. I mentioned an example of that, when Grandshaykh rejected our visit because we quarreled with our mother.

One of my cousins in Lebanon played with a gun and a bullet came in his stomach, which made thirty-six holes in his intestines! Immediately he was rushed to the hospital and doctors said they will try their best but they don't think he will survive until morning. We rushed immediately to Grandshaykh and were there within two hours of that accident. Mawlana Shaykh Nazim was sitting there. Grandshaykh said, "Don't worry, saved." What does "saved" mean? He is going to die! Thirty-six holes in his intestines. He said again, "Saved, we changed his intestine. Go back, don't worry! Tell them."

Mawlana Shaykh Nazim was translating. He said, "Sit here." We were shaking, anxious to go back to see the outcome. He said calmly, "Sit here now and eat." Grandshaykh likes always ground meat with onion and tomato, slow cooked in the oven or over the fire. He made us that, and we ate. We wanted to eat quickly and drive back, but he said, "Eat slowly, don't worry about it. Saved." Then he opened a *ṣuḥbah*! His talks are normally three hours long.

*SubhānAllāh*! Mawlana Shaykh Nazim translated, not missing a word. Grandshaykh speaks for five minutes non-stop, and Mawlana Shaykh Nazim used to try to stop him in order to translate, but he continued. Then Mawlana Shaykh Nazim had to follow quickly to explain, and then he cut him in the middle of the explanation, going to another explanation, and Mawlana Shaykh Nazim was able to continue all the way to the end!

So, after that we returned to Beirut, reaching at midnight. The operation was over and my cousin was speaking under anesthesia, a little bit drowsy. He said, "Don't worry! Don't worry! Grandshaykh was here. He performed my operation." He saw Grandshaykh touching him. Doctors were shocked that he survived. Forty-five years later, he is still alive.

So a *murshid* is not like us. Some people take permission to lead *dhikr* and they make themselves guides. Guides of a what? Guides of their egos! Allāh ﷻ rewarded them because they did something good, and Mawlana gave you authority to take care of people—not to guide, but to take care of them. Try your best *alḥamdūlillāh* and if you progress, you might become a guide, who knows? But, we must not give our egos acknowledgement by saying, "I am a guide," no. We must say, "I am under the feet (of that one)," as we must feel we are nothing, not even an ant, as ants speak.

> *Till, when they came to the valley of the ants, one of the ants said, "O ants! Enter your dwellings, lest Sulaymān (Solomon) and his hosts crush you, while they perceive not.*
>
> *Sūratu 'n-Naml (The Ant), 27:18*

Once Sayyīdīnā Abū Yazīd al-Bistāmī ق saw an ant moving. He stopped addressing his people and said, "Look, it's moving, coming, finding food there, picking up the food, carrying it, and going back. Then a huge line of ants follow. Which language do they speak? What intelligence does the ant use to find food? You cannot find food on this carpet, but if you bring an ant it will find it."

Allāh gave ants that technology, a heavenly sensor. One ant said, "Oh ants, run to your cave before Sayyīdīnā Sulaymān's army steps on you." She knew he is a prophet, a king who represents Allāh ﷻ on Earth, His *khalīfah*. How she knew all that, and we are not able to distinguish who is a real guide from a false guide? Sometimes when we refer to our teachers as the "*khalīfah*" or "shaykh" to show respect, and that is permitted. But the one who is praised, who people think is a guide, you must have that power to say, "I am not that one." Step on your ego!

Every day in the live broadcast (on Sufilive.com), Mawlana Shaykh Nazim says, "I am nothing. I am the weakest one. I am not speaking, but they are making me to speak. I know nothing." Who can say that? Speakers address whole conferences and say, "I am the greatest," but never do they say, "I am the worst! I know nothing."

Grandshaykh said Murshid at-Taṣfīyyah has an obligation from his guide, Murshid at-Tarbīyyah, the sulṭān. He said, "I have an obligation that I must not allow any bad inspiration to come to my heart. All inspiration has to be heavenly and nothing goes in my heart except Allāh ﷻ." And if the door of heavens are open to him to enter, he must close his eyes from entering. Why? Because you must not be occupied with anything created; you must only be occupied with the Creator.

This has a very subtle meaning. Grandshaykh ق says, they open to him to see what's in the heavenly route, but he must not pay attention to it, but only pay attention to the Divine Presence. Heavens are created; Allāh ﷻ is the Creator. Grandshaykh says Murshid at-Taṣfīyyah's intention is to reach Sayyīdinā Muhammad ﷺ, and that his shaykh, Murshid at-Tarbīyyah, can guide him through that light.

## More Characteristics of Murshid at-Tasfiyyah

Grandshaykh ق continues his description, saying Murshid at-Taṣfīyyah must have *malakah,* the capability to purify his *murīds* from 800,000 faults, and he must carry that responsibility on himself to the presence of Prophet ﷺ, even if that *murīd* commits all those sins in one day!

So this gives us an idea of where people stand. Everyone cannot become a guide; it's impossible. Grandshaykh, may Allāh bless his soul, wants to show how deep our faults are engraved within us, that we are not able to see them. Even the tongue cannot express them and pull them out. It needs the vision of the guide. With the eyes of the power he inherits from Prophet ﷺ, he is able to see these mistakes and faults that cannot be seen by everyone. They are above the faults and mistakes that we see in one another. For example, if you look at me you might see some mistakes, and if I look at you, I might find some mistakes. But mistakes that cannot be seen or found, *awlīyāullāh* can see them and remove them.

So that guide has the ability to remove and carry 800,000 faults the tongue cannot describe. Furthermore, he has his company, his association. When he says, *ṭarīqatuna aṣ-ṣuḥbah wa 'l-khayru fī 'l-jamʿīyyah,* "Our way is *ṣuḥbah*" (the gathering), and the company is *wa 'l-khayru fī 'l-jamʿīyyah,* "The best is within the group", that *ṣuḥbah* and company is with each other. But his company is not only with his *murīd*: one face is with his *murīd,* one face is in the company of Prophet ﷺ, and also with alive and deceased *awlīyāullāh.* He can reach them and get power from them any time he wants. That is the third level of *murshid.*

This is a small example quoted from Grandshaykh ق that we can use to examine anyone who claims they have that power. Who has that? That's why they have to be very careful.

When we are in a country, a city, or a village—and there is someone representing *awlīyā*—we have to be careful to understand that he is not the guide. He is conducting the *dhikr,* he is giving *bayaʿ* on behalf of the shaykh, but he is not the guide. The guide is the one who authorized him with that *dhikr* and that *bayaʿ*, but that representative is not the guide. We are traveling around the world and seeing too much of this problem and sickness appearing everywhere.

When the guide connects himself with the association of Prophet ﷺ and with alive and deceased *awlīyāullāh,* immediately they will connect him, and through their power he will be able to see the breaths going in and breaths going out. We say, "Human beings are between two breaths." If Allāh stops one of them, we die. If you cannot inhale and exhale oxygen, you die; that power is taken away. So we are between these two breaths. This is very, very important. Not everyone can understand *awlīyāullāh.* It's very difficult to explain what they say. An entire book can be written from just one word.

Grandshaykh ق said, between these two breaths there are 24,000 wisdoms the *murīd* receives in his heart, and Murshid at-Taṣfīyyah will allow him to see only 12,000 wisdoms; the other 12,000 are hidden from him, because the guide is still in the third level and not in the fourth. So this means when anyone breathes in and out, there are 24,000 wisdoms Murshid at-Taṣfīyyah observes. Allāh knows what these are; they are beyond our mind. Do we know what is going on between the inhalation and exhalation? What kind of angelic, heavenly power is there? What kind of *dhikr* Allāh is causing your soul to do within these two breaths, and with what massive speed? No one knows. No one knows. This is the state of *kamālu 'l-'ubūdiyya*, "Perfect Absolute Worshipness."

Allāh assigns angels to followers in the Naqshbandi Order. Others may speak about their orders and we have respect for them; however, in the Naqshbandi Order there are 24,000 *'ibādah* (acts of worship) within these two breaths that angels perform on your behalf, without you even knowing. This is one of the 24,000 wisdoms which Mawlana Shaykh Nazim is opening now!

Allāh assigned angels between these two breaths: one group of angels bringing the breath in and another taking the breath out. They do *'ibādah,* praising Allāh ﷻ, which is written for you as perfect *'ibādah* (worshipness), not imitational worship. Grandshaykh says, Murshid at-Taṣfīyyah can see those wisdoms; he is able to check on them and can open them to the *murīd's* heart from these 12,000 breaths. That's why in meditation they teach you to breathe in and out. *Awlīyāullāh* know what kind of secrets there are between these two breaths, and we don't know.

Murshid at-Taṣfīyyah is also able to pull out 24,000 oceans of knowledge from every letter in the Holy Qur'an. He can go into any ocean, and every letter is an ocean. You cannot see its depth. It is very deep. Every time that letter is near, they can go inside and pull out 24,000 oceans of knowledge and pour them into the heart of their *murīd*. Grandshaykh ق also said, Allāh will enable them to understand nineteen meanings from every word of the Holy Qur'an as soon as they read it. For example, Allāh said to Adam ﷺ, "I am blowing in him from My soul". He said *nafakhtu*, meaning "I blow". From that one word, they can take nineteen different meanings, in addition to the 24,000 oceans of knowledge in each letter.

## Obligations and Forbiddens

Murshid at-Taṣfīyyah is always on the right path of sincerity and piety. During the day and the night, he will observe and do the 500 obligations that Prophet ﷺ explained and which are mentioned in the Holy Qur'an. He has to do them one-by-one, in his day and in his night, not to leave one behind, not even using *miswāk* to clean his teeth. So what are we doing? We have a turban, a turquoise ring, a *miswāk*, modest clothes, beads, and we say we are following *sunnah*; we are keeping five *sunnah* and we're relieved. Murshid at-Taṣfīyyah keeps the 500 obligations daily! Who is doing that?

Many times when he was young, I slept in the same place with Mawlana Shaykh Nazim. The first time I slept near him, I saw that before he woke up, before he even opened his eyes, he made *tayammum*[13] on the bed, then he put his hand under the pillow. I wondered what he was doing. He put his hand under the pillow, took something and ate it, then he opened his eyes. I asked Mawlana, "What is that?" He said, "This is a *sunnah* of Prophet ﷺ and it's from the 500 obligations." I asked him to explain.

---

[13] An alternate ritual ablution performed in the absence of water.

Mawlana Shaykh said, at night you sleep with *wuḍū* and you're clean, but during the night lots of negative energies are passing through the place where you sleep. That negative energy is bad reflections that move with different kinds of waves and pass over you, but since your eyes are closed, they don't affect you. When you open your eyes, immediately the eyes attract them in and they go through your system. And when this happens, many times you wake up with no energy, depressed, feeling sick, headache, many problems; lots of people come like that. He said the way to purify ourselves and throw away these negative energies, "As Grandshaykh ق taught me, I'm now teaching you."

That's why I say people who don't know, you need a lot of experience with the master as these things don't come easily. Young people can be trained from an early age. When you are young the bad energy does not affect you too much, but when you reach fifty years or older, you're already advanced in problems and sicknesses that become difficult to cure due to all these accumulated bad energies. That's why people sometimes go to psychiatrists. They have been under the radiation of bad energy flying everywhere at night. When they visit the psychiatrist to get help they may even contaminate the psychiatrist, after which they both need purification!

Grandshaykh, may Allāh bless soul, told me to keep on the side of the bed under the pillow, or on the side table, a little bit of salt or a small piece of bread. But we must remember he also said to make *tayammum,* because you should not eat without ablution. After he made *tayammum,* Mawlana Shaykh put that bite of food in his mouth, so you also have to be careful on that issue. People today eat without *tayammum* or ablution; they don't care. Their food is already mixed with all kinds of bad energies. So Mawlana Shaykh puts salt in his mouth, but you can eat anything—a cracker, a piece of bread, an olive, whatever you want—then you can open your eyes. As soon as the food enters the mouth, it becomes a blockage against any kind of bad energy that is floating around anywhere.

That bite will go through your system immediately. Three-hundred angels will put it in your mouth and are responsible for it to pass through your digestive system. I don't know why we didn't mention it before. I never mentioned it to anyone since I went to America twenty years ago! Now after twenty years, Mawlana opened this knowledge again, so try to remember it, in order for these bad energies to be blocked from reaching you.

He said this is one of the 500 obligations. Imagine how many of these 500 we are missing, what we are not doing! So that *walī* has to perform these 500 obligations completely and he has to stop doing 800 forbidden actions. For example, men or women walking on the street, where must your eyes be looking? Your eyes must look to where you are putting your feet; you cannot look far. This is to prevent you from looking at something that is forbidden. When you look around, you might witness sins being committed. But if you are driving a car, you have to look or you will make an accident! Grandshaykh ق said that if you can stop your eye from committing even one of these sins, it is better to Allah ﷻ and He will reward you more for that than if you have performed all the 500 obligations! It's that easy! It is very simple for you as *ʿibādah* (worship).

Look at Allāh's mercy. He says to you, "Don't look at that *ḥarām* (forbidden)." If you see something forbidden, turn your gaze away and immediately say, "A*staghfirullāh*!" You will be rewarded more than if you complete the 500 obligations. To avoid that one time is as if you fulfilled the 500 obligations in the same moment, and you will be rewarded for them. One forbidden you stop yourself from committing is better than the

500 obligations. See how much Allāh is rewarding human beings without them knowing and feeling anything!

This is why I'm saying—I don't want to say it, but I have to—that Prophet ﷺ prohibited someone to look at the face of an *amrad* (a young man with no hair on his face); it is *ḥarām* (forbidden). But, there is an out here, an exit, so don't worry too much. Here *"amrad"* means someone that has no hair completely, hair doesn't grow, so his face looks like the face of a woman. But some of them have traces of hair, in which case it's okay. But *amrad* means someone that has absolutely no hair on their face. In some countries some men naturally only have one or two hairs and they do not shave it, to show they have a beard, according to the Sunnah

These are very subtle, important teachings that we are not learning nowadays. We don't know them and we are thinking that everything is easy. No, it's not easy. Guides are not easy shaykhs. But now today, Mawlana Shaykh Nazim has so much mercy in his heart, he is not pointing out these issues; he allows others to point them out because they will get the sticks (take the blame of people). He does not mention these things, but this is a problem guides are facing, of which students are unaware.

So Murshid at-Taṣfīyyah has the power through Allāh and through Prophet ﷺ and *awlīyāullāh* to put in his *murīd's* heart the 500 obligations as if the *murīd* has done them, and also as if the *murīd* has abandoned the 800 forbiddens completely. The shaykh presents the *murīd* to Prophet ﷺ as if they have done these obligations and they are rewarded for it. The shaykh is doing it on their behalf and he is making *istaghfar* (asking forgiveness) on their behalf when they are committing any of the 800 forbiddens. He has to take away from your heart the 800 forbiddens, as if you have seen them and stopped yourself from committing those sins.

That is not easy! Who can control himself in 24 hours by not committing any sins? Even if you lock yourself in a room for 24 hours, you are committing an infinite number of forbiddens. One may say, "Oh, I locked myself in a room, I'm good." That is a forbidden by itself, to say, "I locked myself in the room. I'm not going to talk to anyone." That is from ego; you are proud of yourself, which is a sin. That is why Prophet ﷺ said, "What I fear most for my *Ummah* is the hidden *shirk*," which is in everyone. Hidden *shirk* is *rīyā*, to do things to impress others. We don't feel them, but they affect all human beings.

Grandshaykh ق said, the shaykh has to eliminate 800 forbiddens from the heart of the *murīd*, according to what Allāh ﷻ likes and what Prophet ﷺ likes. Also, he will give you the power to learn about and understand each of the 800 forbiddens. Anyone who questions how that can be did not yet reach that level of knowing what the *murshid* can put in your heart! So how are you thinking you are a *murshid* when even this much you cannot understand?

When the *murshid* puts in your heart to block these 800 forbiddens, he will give you a meditation, a mantra or focused thought about every forbidden; at that moment, in your heart you will realize it. This is only for the cream of the *murīds*, not for every *murīd*. As you ascend levels, first you were under Murshid at-Tabarruk, the Guide of Blessings, then you were under Murshid at-Tazkīyyah, the Guide of Purification. Now we are discussing the character of Murshid at-Taṣfīyyah, the Guide of Sifting, who collects the cream. In every level the number of *murīds* decreases. The third level is limited to very few people who can understand what the guides are putting in their hearts. They realize the good from the bad, and know the shaykh put the good in their heart and eliminated the bad.

## The Disciple and the Rat

Grandshaykh ق said, Sayyīdinā ʿAbdul-Khāliq ق put a *murīd* in seclusion for forty days and told him, "If something strange happens, tell me." Everyday they sent him one small bowl of lentils. When you eat less you'll be alert as you cannot sleep. When you eat too much, you sleep without feeling. One day, the *murīd* in seclusion told the shaykh, "Oh my shaykh! Today I had something strange happen to me. A rat was speaking to me in perfect Arabic." It's nice for a rat to speak Arabic. It's good, because in *khalwah* (seclusion) everything is possible; don't think it's too much.

Shaykh ʿAbdul-Khāliq al-Ghujdawānī ق said, "What happened?"

"*Yā Sayyīdī*," said the *murīd*, "When you sent me the food, I started eating but the prayer time came. This rat came from the hole in the wall; I was praying and seeing. I wanted to finish quickly because that rat was eating the food. As soon as I completed the prayer, I ran to the rat and it went back in the hole. Then I put a paper to close the hole and continued my prayer. The rat pushed the paper and came another time to eat, then ran away. When I quickly finished my prayer and kicked the rat out, it ran to the hole and stuck its head out, saying in perfect Arabic, 'Oh idiot! Do you think if my name was not written on that food, I would be able to touch it?' Oh my shaykh, this is the strangest thing that happened to me."

Sayyīdinā ʿAbdul-Khāliq al-Ghujdawānī ق said, "Oh my son, you have failed your test, because your *amānat* (trusts), your secrets were going to be given to you, but you blocked them."

"Oh, I didn't do anything", said the *murīd*.

His shaykh said, "Oh my son, do you think the rat can speak Arabic? You must not see the rat, you must see the one behind the rat. It was telling you that you did something wrong. You must let that rat eat because that food is written for it. I was ready to give you your trusts, but *awlīyāullāh* prohibited me, saying, 'No, he's not ready yet,' because you didn't see me, your shaykh, in that rat."

That's big. He's showing him even to that small detail *awlīyāullāh* are observing their *murīds*. Every detail they know, but sometimes they don't talk. You think Mawlana doesn't know about this air conditioner here, and that they don't open it? *Awlīyāullāh* keep quiet. But we have permission to not keep quiet, rather, to criticize. If there is no permission to criticize, we keep our mouth zipped. To this extent *awlīyāullāh* observe their followers in every moment of their lives. Grandshaykh ق used to say, "When you move right or left when you are sleeping in the bed, I can hear your movement stronger than thunder. I can hear that movement of my *murīd*, even if he is in the East and I am in the West."

So, they put in your heart this knowledge of knowing these forbiddens one by one. Mawlana Shaykh Nazim, may Allāh give him long life, told me Grandshaykh ق ordered him into seclusion for six months in Madīnatu 'l-Munawwarah, *'alā sakini afzalu as-Ṣalātu was-salām*. He was ordered to do the five prayers in Masjid an-Nabawi ﷺ in Rawdatu 'sh-Sharīf, so he has to go early for every prayer. That was a long time ago, not so crowded like now. Going to the *masjid* he had to look only at his steps, where he is putting his feet, and he cannot look further. Going, praying, and coming back; continuing like that throughout his seclusion.

At the beginning of the seclusion, he said to me that he got an order to identify as many as he can from the 800 forbidden actions. He was young and it was his second seclusion. His first seclusion was in Amman, Jordan, in a place called Swueileh. We are speaking about his second seclusion, which was for six months in Madīnatu 'l-Munawwarah. He said, "I was thinking how many forbiddens I can count. I began, I was going, thinking. Ah, how is it possible? There are 800 forbiddens… it's too much, how can we count?" We can count two, three, four, five, six, seven, eight, nine, ten; but it's 800!

Mawlana Shaykh said, "I began to count everyday whatever Allāh opened to me in my heart through Prophet ﷺ and my shaykh. By the end of the seclusion six months later, I was able to count 187 forbiddens; understanding them and knowing their remedies, to give medication to these forbiddens to eliminate them. But I was not able to go more than 187. In the beginning I was able to count 30 maximum. One week later they gave me a push and then I was able to count more and more, until they came to 187. After three months they opened for me to know the 800 forbiddens, to teach to the hearts of Mawlana's students."

Mawlana Shaykh Nazim continues, "I'll give you an example. One time, Sayyīdinā ʿAbdul-Qādir Jilānī ق was walking with his *murīd* by the river." I mentioned that story in London recently. But always you reveal or keep things hidden according to the listeners; you don't open everything. "He was walking with his student by the Euphrates to the two rivers. They were passing by a hill and the student didn't know how to swim. As they were moving, he pushed his student with his hand and the student was falling into the river."

## Five Levels of the Heart

According to *awlīyāullāh*, there are five levels in the heart. The first level is called, "the Heart". Here, Shayṭān can come in for bad inspiration, bad gossips, or bad thoughts. *Dunyā* comes in, nafs comes in, and *hawā* (desires) come in; all in the first level. Only certain levels of *awlīyāullāh* can enter the second level, which is called, "the Maqām As-Sirr", the Secret. That *maqām* is in everyone's heart, but no one can access it without the code. Allāh gave these codes to the Prophet ﷺ, who gave them to *awlīyāullāh* who are responsible for this second level; they can access the hearts of their *murīds*. The third level is especially for Naqshbandi Ṭarīqah guides, not for anyone else; Allāh gave them that level. The second level is for other *tariqahs,* and the third level is for *awlīyāullāh* of the Naqshbandi Ṭarīqah; they can access Maqām Sirr as-Sirr, "Secret of the Secret", and they can zoom into "the Secret" and go deep inside.

When you have a circle and you zoom in straight-forward, you come to the center, is it not? The center is a small, very small dot. But if you put a microscope on that small dot, it becomes a huge universe, another face, another level. Like you take blood from someone, you put one little drop inside and look in the microscope. You can see millions of bacteria, a huge universe by itself. A cell of the body is a huge universe. Any cell of the body has its own mechanism, like a huge army battalion against any bacteria that defends the body. So when *awlīyāullāh* zoom inside the Secret, they go to another universe which is "Secret of the Secret", a huge universe in front of them. They see more of the human being's characters and are looking into the wild characters and behaviors we carry. They want you to reach Maqām al-Iḥsān, the Station of Moral Excellence.

But *awlīyāullāh* have a level they cannot go beyond. So it ends, and then it comes to the level of Prophet ﷺ, Maqām al-Akhfā or Maqām al-Khafā, the Hidden State, where Prophet ﷺ can zoom in. It gives him ﷺ the whole picture of Creation, and *awlīyāullāh* cannot enter there. Then there is the fifth level, which is only in Allah's hand; even Prophet ﷺ doesn't go there without permission: Maqām al-Akhfā. So, these are the five levels.

Sayyīdinā ʿAbdul-Qādir Jilānī ق was looking from the second level, from Secret. He pushed his *murīd,* who fell down all the way without *any* doubt about the shaykh; he had complete love, submission, and surrender to the shaykh at that moment. When the shaykh saw him clean, he caught him with his hand under the *murīd's* feet, pulled him back to the hill, and gave him his Trust. Grandshaykh ق said, at that moment *awlīyāullāh* from the Naqshbandi level said to Sayyīdinā 'Abdul-Qādir Jilānī ق, "Why did you give him his Trust?" Shaykh 'Abdul-Qādir said, "I didn't detect anything wrong in the second level." They said, "But we detected on the third level that he did something wrong." A Naqshbandi shaykh would not have given that *murīd* his Trust.

I am asking viewers of this *ṣuḥbah* (on Sufilive.com) who consider themselves huge guides, like a king has a huge kingdom consisting of his ministers, cabinet members, and an army inside the fences. At the door of the fence, there is one person sitting on a chair. He begins to think he is the king. He begins to say, "Oh, I am the best one! I open the door, I have secrets!" Those with permission or authorization to conduct *dhikr* they think they have become guides! If they are guides, can they detect above Sayyīdinā 'Abdul-Qādir Jilānī ق, the *ghawth* of his time? Can they detect what happened in the heart of his *murīd*? Did they reach that level? *Allāhu Akbar!*

That's why sicknesses are too much now, and you find *ḥubb ur-riyāsah,* love to be presidents glued to the chair, what these pseudo representatives aspire to! I'm not saying this out of hate, no; I am saying it out of love. Correct yourself! Tell your followers that you have nothing! When Mawlana Shaykh gives these *ṣuḥbah* everyday live on the Internet, he says, "I'm the weakest, I'm nothing, I'm zero." If Mawlana Shaykh Nazim says that about himself, where is your authority to say you are something? You walk like a peacock, which is the house of Iblīs.

So the Naqshbandi guide was on the Level of Irshād, the highest level, because of the auspicious Golden Chain. In the time of Sayyīdinā 'Abdul-Qādir Jilānī ق they had an association every night with Prophet ﷺ, all of the *awlīyāullāh,* with no discrimination between shaykhs from other *tariqahs* and from the Naqshbandi Ṭarīqahs; everyone had his name where he must be present, to stand or to sit in the presence of Prophet ﷺ.

The Naqshbandi shaykh from the Golden Chain said, "*Yā Sayyīdī*, Shaykh 'Abdul-Qādir Jilānī ق, how you gave him the Trust?"

Shaykh 'Abdul-Qādir Jilānī ق replied, "I didn't detect anything."

"We detected", the Naqshbandi shaykh said.

Shaykh 'Abdul-Qādir Jilānī ق asked, "What you detected?"

"We detected, when he was falling down," said the Naqshbandi shaykh, "he was not objecting. But for us, it was an objection. He was saying, 'With what wisdom my shaykh pushed me in the water?' In Naqshbandi Ṭarīqah that is a question mark, an issue that will prevent him from getting his Trust. If he did not have that complaint, which is how we consider it, he would have already passed from the Secret to the Secret of Secrets, and we would have given him all those trusts from that level, but now we cannot."

What did the *murīd* say? He didn't say anything! He thought, "With what wisdom my shaykh pushed me?" He didn't say, "Why he pushed me!" He only thought, "I want to know the wisdom because I am happy." He was submitting to the push of the shaykh into the river, and he knows he can't swim. He didn't say, "I'm going to die; my shaykh pushed me to get rid of me!" Many of us say, "The shaykh is not seeing us, he wants to get rid of us." Or, "I'm not coming back because I didn't see the shaykh."

It's a blessing when you carry the name of your father. If you don't carry the name of your father, it means you are an illegitimate child, is it not? If you don't know your father, you are an illegitimate child. If you know your father, then you are a legitimate child. You are proud if your father is someone important, an honorable person in the tribe or community, is it not? And what do you think if your father is a saint, a spiritual father, that you call yourself by his name? Is it not a high level? It's enough for us; we are dignified with Mawlana Shaykh's name. For people to say, "These people are Naqshbandi-Haqqani."

When we did our first website in 1990, there were five websites on the Internet. Not Naqshbandi websites; there were CNN, AT&T, corporate news agencies. We were considered the fifth between the best websites; this was in the beginning of 1991, and all of them were linking with us. We were called "Naqshbandi Sufi Order." Then we found out that there are many people who call themselves Naqshbandis, but they are not with Mawlana Shaykh. So then we began to put "Haqqani", which is Mawlana's title. We were the first to use it. "Naqshbandi-Haqqani" was used to say we are a different branch. Like Naqshbandi-Mujaddidi of Sayyīdīna Aḥmad al-Farūqī as-Sirhindī ق. This was to show there is another branch, another line, in order to separate from the others and for everyone to know his father. So we were proud, honored, and dignified to be using "Haqqani" because it is our father's title. Even if you don't see Mawlana Shaykh, you must be proud that he accepted you and you are within his territory. His territory is not this mosque, but the whole world! And the whole world is not his territory, because Allāh gave *awlīyāullāh* access to heavens!

## Seeing the Signs of Allāh's Oneness

So they raised Mawlana Shaykh Nazim up to all 800 forbiddens at the completion of his seclusion. He was able to know and differentiate them one-by-one, and give remedies for each one. Just like a doctor gives you different medicines, he will give you different things. And he said the guide of the third level is able to take 350 signs from the Moon alone, 350 signs of Allāh's Oneness. It means that he is able to see different things that NASA is not able to see. Also, he is able to take ten times more than that from the existence of the Sun.

Imagine the center of the Sun and its surroundings, hundreds of miles from the center. The temperature is 50 million degrees Celsius! When they cremate a dead body at a temperature of 3,000 or 2,000 degrees, the bones and the body disintegrate; nothing will be left, everything will be ashes. At 5,000 degrees, iron and gold melt. At 50 million degrees Celsius, everything falls apart! At 5,000 degrees Celsius, the Earth melts. At 50 million degrees, how is the Sun still standing? A volcano which is 5,000 degrees Celsius under the Earth is shooting and blowing lava out and making everything into ashes.

If two or three times the heat of that volcano comes on Earth, what will happen? It will explode. What kind of matter does the Sun have? We don't know. No one knows; *ʿulamā* don't know, but *awlīyāullāh* know, that's why they can take big signs from the Sun about Allāh's Oneness.

Everything in this universe shows different signs of Allāh's Oneness. Take the leaf of the tree; it shows you many signs of Allāh's Oneness. Is a leaf living? How is it living? Water comes in it. What kind of valve does it have? It turns carbon dioxide into oxygen through the leaves, then it dies and falls down. Allāh is *Yuḥīy wa Yumīt*: He creates and He takes away.

The leaf gives you oxygen to breathe. This is a sign of Allāh's Oneness, one leaf that you don't pay attention to. You step on it with your feet when you are walking. You know that to step on a leaf intentionally is one of the 800 forbiddens? Because that is Allāh's Light! Allāh created that leaf. It's been created by Allāh ﷻ; no one created the leaf except Him, so when you step on a leaf intentionally, that is a sin. But if you are working in the jungle or in a garden and you step, that's okay. But if it's intentional, that is not accepted. How many people throw food in the garbage? Don't ask!

*Awlīyāullāh* can take signs and information from the Moon, from the Sun, and from the stars, and one sign does not interfere with the other. They can take an infinite number of signs from everything around them and understand Allah's Oneness. Murshid at-Taṣfīyyah can observe the reality of the Ocean of Qudrah, Power, because Allah ﷻ is al-Khāliq wa 'l-Qādir, the Creator and the All-Powerful. He has the power to create and the power to do anything He likes, continuously.

Allah ﷻ gave to Prophet ﷺ the manifestation of the Beautiful Names and Attributes, "al-Khāliq", and "al-Qādir" that Prophet ﷺ gives to Murshid at-Tarbīyyah, the guide at the highest level of *irshād*, who gives it to Murshid at-Taṣfīyyah, the guide who sifts the cream, the best of *murīds*. They give him the power to see the signs of Allāh's Oneness within every *murīd* and every person. That's why they don't like students to criticize each other because they see Allāh's Oneness in everyone. They like to bring out the good characteristics in their students and bring down whatever wild characteristics they have, in order to clean that servant from hidden *shirk*, that tendency to put themselves as partner with Allāh ﷻ. For such guides there is no partnership; they can see everything clean and they can understand the reality of the Oneness of Allāh ﷻ.

Murshid at-Taṣfīyyah is able to open the hearts of listeners and observers through the five levels of the heart, until he takes them to the level of:

> *Thumma sawwāhu wa nafakha fīhī min rūḥih.*
> *Then He (Allāh) fashioned him in due proportion, and breathed into him the soul."* *Sūratu 'l-Sajdah (The Prostration), 32:9*

Allāh ﷻ blew that *rūḥ*, what we can describe as His spirit or energy or light, into Sayyīdīna Adam ﷺ, and then Adam was moving. Murshid at-Taṣfīyyah can spiritually take those who attend his association all the way to be under the manifestation of that power!

He has to know all *awlīyāullāh* by name, which includes their relationship and genealogy all the way back to Sayyīdīna Adam ﷺ. He has to achieve the stations 'Ilmu 'l-Yaqīn (Knowledge of Certainty), 'Aynu 'l-Yaqīn (Eye of Certainty), and Ḥaqqu 'l-Yaqīn (Reality of Certainty). 'Ilmu 'l-Yaqīn is the first level of understanding in the Station of "Murīd."[14] To truly be a *murīd,* one must have achieved that level of knowledge. Today we loosely claim, "We are *murīds* of the shaykh." No, we are still beginners and not yet beginners, we are lovers of the shaykh.

Grandshaykh 'AbdAllāh, may Allāh bless his soul, explains in his notes that 'Ilmu 'l-Yaqīn is the knowledge of *wa 'allamnahu mi-ladunnā 'ilma,*[15] from the famous story in Holy Qur'an about Sayyīdīna Mūsā ﷺ meeting Sayyīdīna al-Khidr ﷺ. Sayyīdīna Mūsā ﷺ and his helper found, *'abda min 'ibādina,* "one of Our servants to whom We taught a heavenly knowledge," and Sayyīdīna Mūsā ﷺ was stunned by that high level of knowledge. A true *murīd* in the Naqshbandi Sufi Order has achieved the first level in those knowledges. Allāh ﷻ gives them drops of knowledge from the secrets from the Ocean of Prophet ﷺ.

After he achieves 'Ilmu 'l-Yaqīn, he has to achieve 'Aynu 'l-Yaqīn. In the initial steps of receiving 'Ilmu 'l-Yaqīn, you will

---

[14] Levels that precede the Station of *Murīd* are: Beginner (*Mubtadi'*), and Prepared (*Musta'id).*

15 "And whom We had taught knowledge from Us." (Sūratu 'l-Kahf, 18:65)

be inspired through hearing. In the level of ʿAynu ʾl-Yaqīn, you begin to see through visions. To establish hearing with sight (connecting audio with video) provides a complete picture. If you see something without hearing, you don't know what's going on, and if you hear without seeing, the picture is not complete. When you both see and hear, then you are established on the first steps of Ḥaqqu ʾl-Yaqīn, the Reality of Certainty. At this station you are certain of what you are speaking, you are not imagining.

I'm sorry to say that today many people, all of us, sit and meditate, and sometimes we have a good connection, but sometimes it's a fuzzy connection. You think you are seeing something real but it is only your imagination, it's hallucination.

To *awlīyāullāh* that is not real and they know Shayṭān is playing with you. Not always the picture is clear because you are not yet in the level of *murīdiyyah,* the real student, which is important because they achieved a certain level that the shaykh accepted them as his student. Nowadays the shaykh accepts everyone as a Lover. When you are a murid, you have established ʿIlmu ʾl-Yaqīn (hearing), and ʿAynu ʾl-Yaqīn (vision), then it becomes reality and you can see what's really happening.

And what I want to say now is not from me, it's from Mawlana Shaykh, and it is very deep. "Murshid at-Taṣfīyyah must have achieved these characteristics, qualifications. Even with all these qualifications, in the Naqshbandi Way he is still considered a beginner in the station of *murīd.*" It means even those shaykhs who were authorized by Naqshbandi shaykhs of the Golden Chain, to bring people to guidance and get the "cream" of students, and hear, and see visions, did not achieve all the levels of *murīd* and they are still in the first level! That explanation shows the level of the Naqshbandi Order.

Someone just asked me, "How do I improve my relation with the shaykh?" First I asked if he had taken *baya*ʿ and he answered, "Not yet. I took *baya*ʿ with someone representing him," and he mentioned the person's name. That was the first mistake. Even if you take *baya*ʿ from a representative, say, "Yes, I took *baya*ʿ from the shaykh," because that *baya*ʿ goes all the way to the shaykh. Why? It is mentioned in Holy Qur'an in the verse of *baya*ʿ:[16]

> *'Inna al-ladhīna yubāyiʿūnaka 'innamā yubāyiʿūna Allāh.*
> *Verily, those who give baya*ʿ *to you (O Muhammad), they are giving baya*ʿ *to Allāh.* *Sūratu 'l-Faṭh (The Victory), 48:10*

Allāh ﷻ revealed to Prophet ﷺ in Holy Qur'an those who are giving him *baya*ʿ are actually giving *baya*ʿ to Allāh ﷻ. Real authorization, *ijāzah,* is given by the shaykh and it descends from the line of the Naqshbandi Golden Chain to one who is respected in the presence of the shaykh and the Prophet ﷺ. So if you take *baya*ʿ from one who is not on that level it means nothing; it does not reach the shaykh, as that person has no true connection with the shaykh. However, when you take *baya*ʿ from someone who is genuinely authorized by the shaykh, your *baya*ʿ goes directly to the shaykh, not to this one or that one.

We see too much sickness today based on this violation of *adab* to the shaykh. You ask someone, "Who is your shaykh?" and he will answer, "Oh, this one." "This one" is not yet able to put a diaper for himself; he cannot clean himself, so how do you have *baya*ʿ with him? We must not make that huge mistake!

---

[16] This verse refers to the historic "Pledge Under the Tree," at Hudaybiyyah outside Mecca in 6 A.H.

So, according to Grandshaykh's explanation of the rank of Murshid at-Taṣfīyyah in the Naqshbandi Order, who is the real *murshid*? Now we come to the real *murshid,* Murshid at-Tarbīyyah, the highest level of *irshād,* which we will discuss further *inshāAllāh.*

May Allāh ﷻ forgive us.

*Wa min Allāhi 't-tawfīq, bi ḥurmati 'l-ḥabīb, bi ḥurmati 'l-Fātiḥah.*
*And with Allāh is success. For the sake of the Beloved, for his sake we recite the opening chapter of Holy Qur'an.*

# *Murshid at-Tarbiyyah: Guide of Education*

*Madad yā Sulṭān al-Awlīyā, Shaykh Muḥammad Nāẓim al-Ḥaqqānī.*
*Madad yā Sulṭān al-Awlīyā, Shaykh ʿAbdAllāh al-Fā'iz ad-Dāghestānī.*

Murshid at-Tarbīyyah is the guide who educates and raises the student in discipline and *adab*, carrying him or her every moment to complete their spiritual training. *Tarbiyyah* means "good manners." Murshid at-Tarbīyyah raises the seeker through their journey in the Gnostic way. He raised the other three levels of *murshids* and his followers through them. He is the last and the highest in the hierarchy in Islamic tradition.

Shaykh Muhiyuddin Ibn al-ʿArabi ق described *insān al-kāmil,* the perfect man, in al-Futūḥāt al-Makkiyyah and in various other books, that in every time there is one Sulṭān al-Awlīyā. Murshid at-Tarbīyyah is that level, the guide of raising humanity up by the power of Sayyīdīnā Muhammad ﷺ. So when one passes away another one comes, which he described as the "Silver Brick." He said, Prophet ﷺ is Sulṭān al-Anbīyā (King of all Prophets), and facing him always there must be Sulṭān al-Awlīyā, who inherits directly from Prophet ﷺ.

## Humility of Murshid at-Tarbiyyah

From humility, Naqshbandi *awlīyāullāh* in this time hide themselves and do not show their miracles or their high station. I mentioned this before, but repeat it now. Shaykh Sharafuddīn, a great shaykh of the Naqshbandi Golden Chain, lived in Rashadiya (now Gunekoy), located three hours from Istanbul. Daghestani shaykhs moved there and Grandshaykh grew up there from age seven, under the guidance of his uncle. Six months before he left *dunyā,* Sayyīdīna Shaykh Sharafuddīn ق was ordered by Prophet ﷺ to extract from Holy Qur'an the names of the 40 *khalīfahs* and 59 deputies of Sayyīdīna Mahdī ﷺ. Each of these 99 representatives is under a manifestation of one of Allāh's Beautiful Names and Attributes.

After completing this task, Shaykh Sharafuddīn extracted many other names, of *Rijāl al-Ishrāqīyyūn, Rijālu 'l-mudabbirūn, al-a'immatal-mudabbirūn,* then *shuyūkh* in Islam, then 313 *awlīyā* of the Naqshbandi Order, and then the 7007 *imāms* of the Naqshbandi Order. He extracted all of them from Sūratu 'l-'Anām:

> *And this was Our argument that We vouchsafed unto Abraham against his people: (for) We do raise by degrees whom We will. Verily, thy Sustainer is Wise, All-Knowing. And We bestowed upon him Isaac and Jacob, and We guided each of them as We had guided Noah aforetime. And out of his offspring, (We bestowed prophethood upon) David, and Solomon, and Job, and Joseph, and Moses, and Aaron, for thus do We reward the doers of good. And (upon) Zachariah, and John, and Jesus, and Elijah: every one of them was of the righteous. And (upon) Ishma'il, and Elisha, and Jonah, and Lot. And every one of them did We favor above other people. And (We exalted likewise) some of their forefathers and their offspring and their brethren. We elected them (all), and guided them onto a straight way.*
>
> *Sūratu 'l-'An'ām (The Cattle), 6:83-87*

Shaykh Sharafuddīn ق dove deep into the ocean of these verses and extracted the names of *awlīyāullāh* and the seventeen prophets from whose descendants they emerged. As time passed he became physically weakened because he was going into such deep meditation of the meaning of this verse, taking every name and its spiritual connection. Grandshaykh has the book in which all the names were recorded, which he authorized me to copy and preserve.

Shaykh Sharafuddīn ق called him, "O ʿAbdAllāh Effendi, my son, that task put too much strain on my heart. I am leaving this *dunyā* and passing this secret to you." Grandshaykh ق did not say anything. The next day Shaykh Sharafuddīn ق said, "*Yā walidī*, oh my son! I am leaving this *dunyā* and by order of Prophet ﷺ I am passing to you the secret of the Golden Chain."

Grandshaykh ق said, "*Yā Sayyīdī*, I respectfully ask to be excused from that position; I don't want it."

Who can say that? The shaykh is giving you secrets, what today we run after! Today if the shaykh gives someone a small piece of paper, they will make it as big as a banner, to say, "Oh, I am this and I am that!" But Grandshaykh ق said, "No, I don't want to." Shaykh Sharafuddīn was wondering why Grandshaykh refused such a high honor, to be chosen to carry that message and to inherit secrets from Prophet ﷺ.

That night, Sayyīdīna Shaykh Sharafuddīn presented the situation to Prophet ﷺ in a vision. Prophet ﷺ answered to him, "*Yā walidī*, ask him what he wants. Why did he refuse?" This is an example for us to learn from.

Shaykh Sharafuddīn asked, "Oh my son! Prophet ﷺ is asking, why you are refusing?"

Grandshaykh ق answered, "*Yā Sayyīdī*, what is the benefit I carry if I have so many lovers sitting in front of me and I cannot put them in my level? If you allow me that anytime, anyone sitting in my association and hearing my talks, my advice, will be placed in the same level as I am, then I will accept. Because I know no one is going to do anything, or behave well, or carry good characteristics, or practice all these *awrād*, because they are lazy. They will not do anything, except stab each other in the back and backbite!"

You are students of one shaykh, which means you are the children of one spiritual father, so what is the benefit of stabbing each other in the back? As soon as we leave this room everyone will revert to his or her wild character. So Grandshaykh ق said, "I don't want it, for what? Unless without looking at their behavior, at their wild characters, I can clean them, put them with same level I am in, then I will accept."

I heard this account directly from Grandshaykh ق, who narrated that Prophet ﷺ said, "*Anā rāḍin, ana rāḍin, ana rāḍin*! I am satisfied, I am satisfied, I am satisfied! That's for him."

With this confirmation, Shaykh Sharafuddīn ق wrote his will and passed it to Grandshaykh ق, saying, "Oh my son, after three days I am leaving *dunyā*. Give this to people and let them hear it, see it." I am speaking now about how much Murshid at-Tarbīyyah must sacrifice. They have no ego, they don't care if you give them the paper or not. Today people are running after papers (documentation), but what is the benefit of taking *ijāzah* if it has no heavenly support? If that does not come from heavens, whatever paper you are getting is only an imitation; even to get papers stamped is an imitation.

Shaykh Sharafuddīn ق gave his will to Grandshaykh, who said, "After, you pass it." That is a real will, like when Grandshaykh 'AbdAllāh al-Fā'iz ad-Dāghestānī wrote his will a week before he passed away, and when he gave to us he said, "You pass it."

People don't know these things. They think these things are easy to acquire, easy to know, easy to learn. You need experience, you need training, which is not only carrying a stick and wearing a turban; that is a false image. You need a spiritual cane against your ego. The cane in the hand is an indication that it has to always hit your ego; that's why we carry a cane. Prophet ﷺ used to carry a cane to put away snakes. Snakes represent the wild character of human beings, so when you carry a cane you carry it against your own ego.

There are shepherds for wild animals and shepherds for domestic animals. Thieves are shepherds for wild animals; they are wild so they can be with wild animals. Hyenas group together and jump on one animal and catch it together, because they are cowards to go by themselves, so they need others around them. Human hyenas recruit people around them in order to make hegemony over everything, here and everywhere. I don't care; if they listen, if they don't listen, no problem.

When Shaykh Sharafuddīn passed away, Grandshaykh took the will. Shaykh Sharafuddīn was lying on the bed and while they were washing him, when they poured the *ghusl* water over his hands, he opened his hands like a scoop and the water trickled out and the *murīds* present drank from it! When they finished washing him, he dropped his hands down. *Allāhu Akbar!* How is that possible? *Awlīyāullāh* are alive in *dunyā* and they are alive in *Ākhirah.*

He gave the will to Grandshaykh before he passed away. When he passed away, Grandshaykh became Shaykh of Golden Chain. What was the first thing he did before calling anyone, asking anyone, or saying anything? What was that? He took the will, tore it apart and threw it in the well, saying, "I don't need anyone to know who I am!" It means he is not after *dunyā,* he is submitting to Allāh ﷻ, and he will see whoever Allāh will send to him from His servants. Grandshaykh ق was not running after people, but people were running after him and those who were sincere he knew would come to him. That's why *awlīyāullāh* don't like to show themselves; they don't want to people to know them and they prefer to remain hidden.

Still today in Rashadiyya, his village in Turkey, they know him as "Hajji 'AbdAllāh," not "Shaykh 'AbdAllāh" even, not "Sulṭānu 'l-Awlīyā," they don't even know he is a *walī.* He hid himself and his ego was finished. Look how Murshid at-Tarbīyyah is in complete submission.

Those who think they are running places for Mawlana, that is rubbish! I was in London last week. They always announce my arrival one week before, to notify people to attend. Imām Zimmer from Kosovo leads Jumuʿah there; Mawlana Shaykh Nazim asked him to do that. After Jumuʿah he announced, "Next week Shaykh Hisham is coming from Cyprus for *daʿwah* and to see people, to give the Jumuʿah *khutbah* and lead *dhikr*."

As soon as he finished that announcement, the hyenas ran after him, saying, "Who gave you permission to announce that?" He said, "Permission for what? I don't need permission as this person is very well-known. He is the son-in-law of Mawlana Shaykh, forget about anything else! He is running from east to west for Mawlana Shaykh. What is your business? You have nothing to do here, all of you are hyenas! Go away from here."

These people want *daʿwah* and *ṭarīqah*? They come begging here at the door of Mawlana Shaykh for everything, and when they go there they become wild animals!

I am asking Allāh to take all of our rights, because we have rights on them. All of us! Mawlana got all those places in London for *daʿwah*, for education, for Islam, for Allāh ﷻ, for Sayyīdīna Muhammad ﷺ, for *awlīyāullāh*, for Sufism, for peace—for sure, not for making business! *Allāhu yumhil wa lā yuhmil.*

A severe punishment is coming and we don't want them to be punished in *dunyā*, no, let them enjoy it. We want their punishment in *Ākhirah*. We want to take all their *ḥasanāt* in *Ākhirah*, it's our right. If they don't know Sharīʿah, let them read what happens to those who backbite, and what are the rights of those who are backbitten, then they will know the seriousness of what they are doing! It is better to take your rights in *Ākhirah*, as to Allāh ﷻ *dunyā* does not have the value of the wing of a mosquito. Prophet ﷺ was abused in *dunyā*. No problem, let them abuse, Allāh will open another door.

But a Day is coming when everyone will run from his brother, his father, his mother, his wife, his children. At that time everyone has a problem to be solved, but he will drop everything and run to be accepted in Paradise! That is the difficult time when Allāh ﷻ will call before Him the oppressors and the oppressed. He will ask the oppressed, "What is your right?" And the oppressed will reply, "*Yā Rabbī,* I want my rights! In *dunyā*, he did this and this and this and this to me!" Allāh ﷻ will take all the oppressor's *ḥasanāt* (good deeds) and give him all the oppressed one's *sayyīāt* (bad deeds) dropped on his head!

Especially those who are responsible for *masājid*, priories, and spiritual places, because if they are doing something wrong it means they are doing wrong to everyone. Count how many have been oppressed, not just one. If they oppressed me, I have behind me many people. So they are going to face a big punishment. May Allāh ﷻ take our rights from them on the Day of Judgment because we don't want it here.

Murshid at-Tarbīyyah is the one who does not show himself as higher than you; he appears as a normal human being who does not want anything. They called Grandshaykh, "Hajji ʿAbdAllāh," the lowest level of respect, although he is Sulṭānu 'l-Awlīyā. May Allāh forgive us.

**Question from a student:** If you are far from the shaykh, what must you do?

**Mawlana Shaykh Hisham:** You don't need to do anything. You need to be a lover, as all of us are lovers in the presence of the shaykh. We love the shaykh and we are beginners. In the shaykh's eyes, he loves all students and followers equally. He does not consider this one is higher or that one is lower. In his presence they are all his children, who will all be in his level on the Day of Judgment; they will not be different but they have to try to progress in *dunyā* to reach as much knowledge and lights as they can. If they reach it, *alḥamdūlillāh,* and if they did not reach it, the shaykh will take them by the hand and pull them to his level, no problem.

However, this honor is reserved exclusively for those who have good hearts and love the shaykh and his *murīds,* but it does not include those who backbite. We are going to ask our rights from them even if they are lovers! We are not forgiving them, because they are damaging Mawlana Shaykh's reputation, *ṭarīqah's* reputation, and everyone's reputation with their wrong actions! Wherever they are and whatever they will become, we don't care for them! We are going forward with this line, Mawlana Shaykh's teachings, and we are not listening to their nonsense.

For example, yesterday one lady said to the other, "Let's come and listen to the *ṣuḥbah.*" The other one said, "Oh, I don't respect Shaykh Hisham." She asked, "Why?" The other replied, "Because for every *baya*ʿ he takes two-hundred dollars." Imagine! This happened here, in Mawlana Shaykh Nazim's *masjid* upstairs. For every *baya*ʿ, I take two-hundred dollars?!! That is a vicious rumor and backbiting. Allāh ﷻ will punish whoever spreads rumors. That and worse happened in Mawlana's mosque here!

May Allāh forgive us and forgive them, and bless those who are on Sufilive watching the broadcast live. May Allāh bless them because they are listening and giving their hearts. May Allāh support them, and support all those here, and keep us all lovers to Mawlana Shaykh Nazim.

## The Station and Powers of Murshid at-Tarbiyyah

Sulṭān al-Awlīyā is the highest above the five *aqṭāb:* Quṭb, Quṭb al-Bilād, Quṭb al-Mutaṣṣarif, Quṭb al-Irshād, and Quṭb al-Aqṭāb. These are the five pillars that Prophet ﷺ authorized to run the affairs of human beings in *dunyā* and in *Ākhirah*. They are responsible for everything, and each has a different level and a different way. Above them is the *ghawth*, who is between the "Pillar of Pillars" and Prophet ﷺ. He is the pipe; the channel. Sayyīdīna Shah Naqshband ق was one of them, as was Sayyid ʿAbdul Qadir al-Jilani ق. From century to century they differ. Above the *ghawth* is Sulṭān al-Awlīyā. The *sulṭān* reached the highest level and there is no one above him except Prophet ﷺ and His companions, and the prophets and messengers. As such, he is the head of *awlīyāullāh*.

> *Prophet ﷺ said, "I am the city of the knowledge and ʿAlī is the door."*

It means there is a city of knowledge that *awlīyāullāh* are trying to take drops from. Sulṭān al-Awlīyā reached the highest level in the ability to discern matters. He acquired all knowledge of ʿIlmu'l-Yaqīn (Certainty of Knowledge), ʿAynu'l-Yaqīn (Certainty of Vision), and Ḥaqqu'l-Yaqīn (Certainty of Reality).

The first level, ʿIlmu'l-Yaqīn (Certainty of Knowledge), is parallel to Maḥabbatullah (Love of Allāh), Maḥabbatu'l-Ḥabīb (Love of Prophet), and Maḥabbatu'l-Mashaykh (Love of the Shaykhs).

The second level, ʿAynu'l-Yaqīn (Certainty of Vision), is parallel with the stations Ḥuḍūrullah (Presence of Allāh), Ḥuḍūru'l-Ḥabīb (Presence of Prophet), and Ḥuḍūru'l-Mashaykh (Presence of the Shaykhs).

The third level, Ḥaqqu 'l-Yaqīn (Certainty of Reality), is parallel with the stations Fanā'un-fillāh (Annihilation in Allah's Divine Presence), Fanā'un fi 'l-Ḥabīb (Annihilation in Prophet), and Fanā'un fi 'l-Mashaykh (Annihilation in the Shaykhs).

What do these levels of knowledge indicate? To achieve the station of 'Ilmu'l-Yaqīn, one has fulfilled all requirements of all knowledge that comes to him through hearing. He can receive knowledge through the inner spiritual ear of the soul. Just as there are a heart and ears in the body, there are a heart and ears in the soul, so he is able to hear with the ears of his soul. Example: is there anyone other than me speaking now? Is there any sound or voice coming from anyone else here? No, but there is a continuous sound from us, although we do not hear it, but they can hear it: the sound of breathing. It becomes so habitual that we stop hearing it, but if you focus you can hear it in the back ground during inhalation and exhalation.

Between these two breaths *awlīyāullāh* can detect up to 24,000 embedded wisdoms, like your identity is embedded in your DNA, the blueprint for your appearance. *Awlīyāullāh* see the spiritual blueprints of your characteristics in your breaths. There are many places in the body where our identity is embedded and encrypted, like in the thumb. All thumbprints contain unique, encrypted knowledge and *awlīyāullāh* can read it.

They hear the breaths and the wisdom encrypted in them. They also hear the energy coming out of you. They hear the gossips that come to your mind, body, and heart. They hear your inspirations, good or bad. Nothing about you is hidden from them; like you are a patient and they are the full hospital, monitoring you every moment. They screen you completely—who you are and what your capabilities are—and they monitor not just you, but every single person, without any overlap or interference, and all are different from each other!

Simple example: Do we see anything here? No. Do we hear anything other than me? Forget about me, no. Turn on an audio recorder or radio, then do you hear something? Yes, you hear electromagnetic waves giving sound, and immediately your ear tunes in to it. How can the radio hear and you cannot hear? Similarly, *awlīyāullāh* detect various waves and turn them into sounds. They can hear and understand everyone with a digital, very high-acuity signal. It's acute, very pure. Recently they discovered a signal that doesn't go in a different short, long, or acute wavelength; it is a straight-line wavelength that can carry everything in it. They are so amazed by it! They are studying it, but cannot understand it now.

Just now, Mawlana said, "Don't be amazed." If you check a patient's heart with an EKG, you can see the different electromagnetic waves running in his heart. But as soon as the person's heart stops, it becomes a flatline, the "wavelength of submission." Allah ﷻ gave power to *awlīyāullāh* to put their students into that wavelength of full submission and present them to Prophet ﷺ.

So as with electromagnetic wavelengths, if a radio can hear and a TV can see, understand that at a minimum, *awlīyāullāh* have that power! They are able to sit anywhere and see everything from us; it reaches them through wavelengths continuously flowing to infinity. *Awlīyāullāh* can see the past because wavelengths continue from the present into the future. Even if you are dead, what you said during your lifetime is continuously going, because wavelengths don't die.

Prophet ﷺ mentioned that when a believer—a pious person who kept his duty to Allāh—is in his grave, he is in *rawḍatan min riyāḍ al-jannah*, inside a garden from the groves of Paradise.

> *The best of asceticism is remembrance of death and the best worship is contemplation, and whoever was burdened by*

*remembrance of death, his grave would be a garden from the groves of Paradise.* *ad-Daylami in* Musnad al-Firdaws

*The grave is a trench from the pits of Hell or it is a garden from the groves of Paradise.* *Bukhārī* and *Muslim*

Allāh ﷻ gives *awlīyāullāh* that ability. So what about Sulṭān al-Awlīyā? Of course, he is following in the footsteps of Prophet ﷺ; wherever Prophet is putting his feet Sulṭān al-Awlīyā is following. All of us must be happy that Allāh ﷻ connected us with a *sulṭān* that can take us to the presence of Sayyīdīnā Muhammad ﷺ!

'Ilmu'l-Yaqīn (Certainty of Knowledge), is the knowledge of the ear. How do you acquire that? You sit in front of your teacher or your father who is speaking and you are hearing. You sit in front of them and listen because you love them. So it means the station of 'Ilmu'l-Yaqīn runs parallel to the stations of Maḥabbatullah (Love of Allāh), Maḥabbatu'l-Habīb (Love of Prophet), and Maḥabbatu'l-Mashaykh (Love of Shaykh).

The next level, 'Aynu'l-Yaqīn (Certainty of Vision), moves parallel to Ḥuḍūrullah (Presence of Allāh), Ḥuḍūru'l-Ḥabīb (Presence of Prophet), and Ḥuḍūru'l-Mashaykh (Presence of the Shaykhs). When you are hearing and seeing, you begin to feel a presence. In the beginning you see a fuzzy picture; there is something there, but you are not yet seeing it clearly. Your vision is like the difference between an untuned analog TV with static reception, then as you progress it becomes clear analog reception, then as you progress further you get a digital reception, and then finally, with even more progress you get high definition.

When *awlīyāullāh* reach the stations of Ḥuḍūrullah, Ḥuḍūru'l-Ḥabīb, and Ḥuḍūru'l-Mashaykh, they have established the knowledge of 'Ilmu'l-Yaqīn and 'Aynu'l-Yaqīn.

When you establish these two, you reach a reality in which you understand you are nothing, you are zero. You cannot consider yourself as existing because one day you will leave this *dunyā* and cease to exist, so existence is only for Allāh ﷻ and you submit in that ocean of *fanā*: Fanā'un fillāh (Annihilation in Allāh's Divine Presence), Fanā'un fi 'l-Ḥabīb (Annihilation in Prophet), and Fanā'un fi 'l-Mashaykh (Annihilation in the Shaykhs).

When they take you to enter that and you submit completely, then you enter the third level, Ḥaqqu'l-Yaqīn, Certainty of Reality. Now you establish a real understanding of everything going on around you. That is a characteristic of Murshid at-Tarbīyyah, that he dwells in the hearts of his students. Prophet ﷺ said:

> *Whatever Allāh put in my heart, I put in the heart of Abū Bakr aṣ-Ṣiddīq.*

It's not that Abū Bakr aṣ-Ṣiddīq was gaining it; no, it was *granted* to him. So, *awlīyāullāh* grant their followers without expecting their followers to do this or that; they pour into their hearts that kind of knowledge.

Murshid at-Tarbīyyah must have that power to pour knowledge into the hearts of his students without any effort on the part of the students, because all of us are lazy! What they pour in your heart is the real knowledge; knowledge that you acquire by yourself is not that important.

> *Is he better, who laid the foundation of his building on piety to Allāh and His Good Pleasure, or he who laid the foundation of his building on an undetermined brink of a precipice ready to crumble down, so that it crumbled to pieces with him into the Hellfire? And Allāh guides not the wrong-doer.*
>
> *Sūratu 't-Tawbah (The Repentance), 9:109*

This means it will fall all the way in Hellfire, so don't build your home on a cliff! By thinking that we are doing something, acquiring and acquiring, our home is built on a cliff. If not for the support of Prophet ﷺ and of *awlīyāullāh* through Prophet, we will fall quickly and immediately, but they carry us. That's why we have to know we are not at those imaginary levels or titles that we give ourselves, because when you build your *ʿibādah* on your ego, it's worthless. Don't live on the edge, live in the middle where it is safe.

## Story of Shaykh Ahmad al-Badawi

Sayyīdīnā Aḥmad al-Badawī ق from Egypt was one of the greatest *awlīyā* in his time. Every year millions of people come to his area to pay tribute and keep the memory of him alive. That area flourished because of him. From his secret, Allāh ﷻ brings these people, *subḥānAllāh.* So, Aḥmad al-Badawī was praying, and praying, and praying, "*Yā Rabbī*, open Your door for me, open Your door for me, open Your door for me! I want to enter Your Divine Presence! Give me the keys, give me the keys!" There was no answer, although he is a *walī*, but one who had not been given the keys. So what about people who think they are *awlīyāullāh,* dispensing "guidance", making themselves shaykhs? They are still in diapers and every moment they need a new diaper as so much sickness is coming from them, non-stop diarrhea from their bad ego's! They contaminate those who follow them by mistake.

Aḥmad al-Badawī ق was the biggest *ʿalim* and biggest *walī* of Egypt, and he was asking, "*Yā Rabbī*, open Your door for me, give me the keys!" When Mawlana says to someone, "Go make *dhikr*," they think themselves so high, they become pharoahs, sitting on their chairs, giving orders. What order you are giving? First order your wife and kids! Fix within yourself first, then look outside!

So, he said, "*Yā Rabbī,* open Your door, open Your door, I need the key, I need the key!" There is no answer, because there is *adab*, discipline that must be observed. You cannot go there and kick the door and come to the presence of the shaykh without *adab*. How many people do that, saying, "Oh, we are his children!" Yes, you are spiritual children of the shaykh, but you have to keep your *adab*. Our way is not that whoever you like you invite and whoever you dislike you reject. Such people do not honor equality; it's not in their dictionary. Only they understand, "myself."

Many people pray, "*Yā Rabbī,* let us see Mawlana." They come from far away, begging, "Can we see Mawlana?" And they return home without seeing him. Never mind. We say, *Allāhu yumhil wa lā yuhmil,* Allāh waits for you (to repent), but never ignores (what you've done), and He will punish the wrongdoers in the end. May Allāh forgive us!

So Aḥmad al-Badawī was asking, asking, asking, when finally he heard a voice, "No!" Then he asked more, "Give me the key, give me the key!"

Then someone in the street appeared in front of him and said, "*Yā* Aḥmad! I have a key for you. You want it?"

He looked at that one, thinking, "What is he saying, 'I have a key for you?'" He said, "What kind of key?"

That one answered, "I have the key you are asking for."

The *ʿalim* looked at him with ignorance, saying, "*Akhī* (my brother)! Who are you? Nothing but a dirty-looking gypsy?"

Prophet ﷺ said:

*It may be that a curly-haired, dusty person asks Allāh for anything; Allāh will respond to him immediately.* *Muslim*

When you look at such a person you feel uncomfortable, like today when we see a homeless person. But if he will ask Allāh ﷻ for something, Allāh will grant his request. Allāh doesn't look at the outside, noticing, "This one is rich, this one is from high society, this one is a prince, a princess, this one is president, this one is a minister." No, Allāh ﷻ looks at the heart. However, today there is a policy of some people to admit only those who are rich into the presence of Mawlana Shaykh, and perhaps those who are not rich can sit only because they are door keepers. But these door keepers are not keeping equality. Think about it.

So that person said, "These are the keys."

Aḥmad al-Badawī ق said, "No, I will not take the keys from you. I want the keys from the Key Maker, from Allāh ﷻ! Who are you? You are like me. I don't take keys from you. I want to take them from Allāh ﷻ."

He Aḥmad al-Badawī ق, who continued, continued, continued asking, "*Yā Rabbī*, give me Your keys, Your keys," until he heard a sound from Heaven, saying, "*Yā* Aḥmad! You want My keys? They are with that person who you have thrown away. Go back and run after the keys."

This *dunyā* is based on the principle of cause and effect. You do something, you get something. So now he is finished, he has to come back and run to get the keys! He was running, running, running, looking where he left that one, that higher *walī* who had been beside him, and he could not find him! For six months he searched, and finally Allāh ﷻ ordered that *walī* to appear to him.

Immediately Aḥmad al-Badawī sees his face and said, "Oh please, I am looking for you!"

He said, "Since when?"

"For six months I am looking. I want my keys. Do you have them?"

He said, "Yes, I have your keys."

"I need my keys, can you give them to me please?"

He said, "No, I am not giving them to you."

"Why not?!!"

"You didn't accept them at the beginning. Now, after you heard an angel tell you the keys are with me, am I going to give them to you for free now? No way! Before, your ego was playing with you and now you are submitting, but just to get the keys. Had you accepted before, I would have destroyed your ego!"

"So, what you do you want?" Aḥmad al-Badawī asked. "I am ready to pay you any price. How much money do you want?"

He said, "No, we are not after money. Throw it away."

You think when you give the *walī* money he cares about it? When people came to Sayyīdīnā 'Umar bin Khattab ﷺ, saying, "*Yā* 'Umar, how you are taking from this person; his money is *ḥarām* for *zakāt*?" He said, "No problem if his money is *ḥarām,* because I give it to poor people who are in need, and it might be Allāh will forgive the one who gave it." Those people are happy because you gave to them. *Awlīyāullāh* don't keep the money you give; they give it to others for your benefit. It is to your disadvantage when you don't give, and some people's hands are trembling when they give!

What was the price of those keys now?

He said, "Give me all the knowledge that you acquired with your ego, because that is not real knowledge. If I give you heavenly knowledge, it will be as if I am building on a cliff; it will fall down."

Aḥmad al-Badawī ق said, "How I can give you my knowledge?"

"For us it is simple, don't worry too much. Look into my eyes."

Aḥmad al-Badawī looked into his eyes and like a magnet, he pulled out all his knowledge, like downloading all embedded knowledge, what is in his mind and heart, until not even knowledge of Sūratu 'l-Fatihah remained! Then he left him, and Aḥmad al-Badawī was roaming the streets. He was Grand Mufti of the area, and now he became the most crazy one that children taunted and threw stones at, saying he was crazy. For six months they left him in that state, torturing his ego, polishing him. Then Aḥmad al-Badawī appeared in front of that *walī*, who said, "*Yā* Aḥmad, now you are ready. Look into my eyes." He looked into that *walī*'s eyes and he was pouring from his heart into Aḥmad al-Badawī's heart heavenly knowledge's, pouring, and pouring, and pouring, and pouring, and finally gave him the keys, his trust. Then he was able to be in the presence of Prophet ﷺ and in the Divine Presence. Then that *walī* left him!

From that moment no one could look into Aḥmad al-Badawī's eyes or face, or they will faint. So he veiled his face with a *niqāb* so no one could see his eyes. If anyone spoke to him they fainted. Until today, the divine light that came to his heart attracts millions of people in Egypt.

Murshid at-Tarbīyyah must have that power to attract; in fact, he has these six realities in his heart:

**The Power of Attraction** of either objects or people to the shaykh—*Ḥaqīqat al-jadhbah;*

**The Power of Emanation** or outpouring of experience from Prophet ﷺ through the chain of transmission to the heart of the disciple—*Ḥaqīqat at-taṣṣaruf;*

**The Power of Alignment** of the shaykh's heart towards the disciple's, and of the disciple's towards his spiritual goal—*Ḥaqīqat at-tawajjuh;*

**The Power of Connection** to divine power and favors through the Golden Chain—*Ḥaqīqat at-tawāssul;*

**The Power of Guidance** to the destination embarked upon through the spiritual connection—*Ḥaqīqat al-irshād;* and,

**The Power of Folding Time and Space**—*Ḥaqīqat aṭ-ṭayy.*[17]

Murshid at-Tarbīyyah has no self, no ego, and he uses all these powers to raise those in his care—lovers, beginners, those who are ready, and *murīds*—to higher spiritual levels. Whatever he says is a truth and the reality.

That's why 200 years ago when Sayyīdinā ʿAbdul-Wahāb ash-Shaʿrānī, one of the greatest scholars and *awlīyā* of Egypt, was asked to explain *ʿilmu 'ẓ-ẓāhir wa 'l-ʿilmu 'l-bāṭin,* the knowledge of what is apparent and what is hidden, he said, "What do you mean by 'hidden'? We don't have hidden knowledge; all our knowledge is *ẓāhir,* external."

They could not understand. Of course he has internal, hidden knowledge, but for *awlīyāullāh* all knowledge is visualized, they can see it, so for them nothing is hidden. He meant, "For us everything is *ẓāhir* for we observe it. For you it is hidden because you are blind." *Awlīyāullāh* have that power of understanding.

---

17 Mawlana Shaykh Nazim's discourse, "The Final Limit" in Mercy Oceans Lovestreams, pp. 101-110.

## Guardian of Your Divine Trust

Another characteristic of Murshid at-Tarbīyyah which Allāh ﷻ opened to him through Prophet ﷺ is that he can see the response souls gave to Allāh ﷻ on the Day of Promises, and what Allāh gave them as their *amānāt*, trust. At that time the human form was not yet created, and Allāh ﷻ gave His trust to heavens and Earth to carry and gave each subtle soul a trust to carry.

> *Truly, We offered al-Amānat, the Trust, to the heavens and the Earth and the mountains, but they declined to bear it and were afraid of Allāh's torment, but Man bore it. Verily, he was unjust (to himself) and ignorant (of its results).*
>
> *Surātu 'l-Aḥzāb (The Confederates), 33:72*

The greatest thing for human beings is heavens and Earth; they see in this universe the greatness of Allāh ﷻ that cannot be defined or limited. Wherever you travel you see the planets and galaxies; you cannot reach their vastness and it makes you feel as if you are nothing, zero, as Mawlana Shaykh is saying here in his notes.

> *Thumma irjiʿ 'l-baṣara karratayni yanqalib ilayka 'l-baṣaru khāsian wa hūwa ḥasīr.*
>
> *Again turn your vision a second time: (it) will come back to you dull and discomfited, in a state worn out. Surātu 'l-Mulk, 67:4*

So, when Allāh ﷻ offered His Trust to the universe and the heavens to carry, they said, "No, *yā Rabbī*, we are afraid to carry it!" Who can carry Allāh's Trust? Allāh is giving us an order through His Prophet, the Seal of Messengers, Sayyīdīna Muhammad ﷺ! But we cannot carry it and people are disobeying because we are weak. So in all their greatness which Allāh ﷻ bestowed upon them, heavens and Earth said, "No, we cannot carry it." Who is higher in creation? Who is more difficult to create, a human being or a universe? Allāh ﷻ said in Holy Qur'an:

> *La-khalqu 's-samāwāti wa 'l-arḍi akbaru min khalqi 'n-nāsi wa lākinna akthara an-nāsi lā ya'lamūn.*
> *The creation of the Heavens and the Earth is indeed greater than the creation of Mankind, yet most of Mankind know not.*
> *Surātu 'l-Ghāfir (Who Forgives, The Clement), 40:57*

So when Allāh offered the Trust to heavens and Earth, they replied, "No, we cannot." They understood, as Allāh said in Holy Qur' an:

> *fa abayna an yaḥmilnahā wa ashfaqnā minhā wa ḥamalahā 'l-insānu innahu kāna ẓalūman jahūla.*
> *But they declined to bear it and were afraid of Allah's torment, but Man bore it. Verily, he was unjust (to himself) and ignorant (of its results).* *Surātu 'l-Aḥzāb (The Confederates), 33:72*

*Insān* is a general term meaning "human beings." So here Allāh ﷻ is saying in general, human beings are oppressors and ignorant, not necessarily to others, but to themselves. Why? Because from kings to presidents to ministers to normal human beings, all are ignorant of Allāh's rights and they are oppressors on themselves because they are not honoring Allāh's rights. Only Sayyīdīna Muhammad ﷺ, prophets, the *Ṣaḥābah* and *awlīyāullāh* are saved; all others are progressing in whatever they are doing, if they are oppressors or not. We are oppressors, *ẓalūma,* and we are ignorant, *jahūla.*

Mostly we are ignorant at the doors of *awlīyā*! *SubhānAllāh!* We are all oppressors and we are all ignorant, but *alḥamdūlillāh,* we are coming here! Allāh is saving us; many are not saved. It means you are more honored to Allāh ﷻ: He is honoring us more than others. To come to *Sayyīdī* Shaykh Muhammad Nazim al-Haqqani ق and to *Sayyīdī* Shaykh

ʿAbdAllāh ad-Dagestani ﻕ is a high honor and we must be happy!

Some come solely for fame; Allāh ﷻ knows what they are coming for, but still they receive mercy. Those who think they are near the shaykh are far away from him, so don't think if you are near the shaykh you are clever!

I will tell you about Sayyīdīna ʿUbaydullāh al-Ahrār ﻕ, the story Grandshaykh ﻕ always mentioned. *Awlīyāullāh* used to speak to scholars, not to people like us, who don't know anything. Mawlana Shaykh Nazim said that when he was younger, all Grandshaykh's associations were with *ʿulamā*, not only *ʿulamā* but with *awlīyā* also. When Mawlana speaks, *awlīyā* are ordered to put their headsets, open their receivers and hear his speech from east to west, wherever they are.

Sayyīdīna ʿUbaydullāh al-Ahrār had a lot of students, many of whom were scholars older than him, very high *ʿulamā* educated in Sharīʿah and *ṭarīqah*. But, everyone has an ego, and some think, "I am sitting besides the shaykh," and another one will say, "I am in front of the shaykh," and another one will say, "I am at the door of the shaykh," still another one will say, "I am sitting with the shaykh in his room," while yet another one will say, "Oh, I prepared the food for him!" Today they feel they are so close to the shaykh, and this is also how they believed in the time of Sayyīdīna ʿUbaydullāh. There is wisdom keeping them like that.

So before he passed away, he said to his *murīds*, "I am giving my will to those who will carry my secret," because the shaykh can have more than one *khalīfah* after him, as he likes. He can have one, two, three, he can even have hundreds; he decides, no one else can decide. He said, "I am living this *dunyā* and I am going to appoint someone to be my *khalīfah*, but I am not going to say his name. When I die, take my turban to my room and throw it up in the air; it will go around, around, around, around, and land on the head of my *khalīfah*."

Remember the *ḥadīth* of Prophet ﷺ about when he arrived in Madinah, he was riding the camel and some people wanted to take him to stay in their homes, and Prophet ﷺ said, "Leave the camel, it is ordered to go where I will stay, it will indicate the place." And the camel stopped at the home of Sayyīdinā Abū Ayyūb al-Anṣārī ؓ.

Similarly, Sayyīdīna 'Ubaydullāh ق said, "My turban will indicate who will be my *khalīfah*." So everyone was happy and hoping the shaykh would die quickly so they might be chosen for that honor. What do you expect? That's why it's *ḥarām* to speak about *khilāfah* when Mawlana Shaykh is still with us, because it's as if you are saying we don't want our shaykh anymore, and that is a big sin! Those who are doing this or that must be very careful; they know themselves and we don't want to mention their names.

So, as the shaykh was passing away he said, "Before you bury me send the turban around." As soon as he passed away they ran, competing with one another for who is going to get the turban first. They got the turban and threw it up in the shaykh's room; it began turning, turning, turning and everyone raised his head for the turban to land on it. There was one person who everyone thought was disgusting, with greasy curly hair, covered with dust, sitting outside at the door taking people's shoes as they enter. He would clean and polish them, and arrange them nicely at the back of the room. No one gave him any attention, because they were big *'ulamā*, representatives of the shaykh, who were authorized to give *baya'*, initiation, and *ṭarīqah*. However, the holy turban landed on that one's head!

They said, "*Oof*! Take that turban away, it's wrong! All the *'ulamā* are here, so this time hold the door so it can't go out and throw the turban inside the room towards them!" They threw the turban again and it was turning, turning, turning in the room, but still went back to that one sitting at the door! Those *ʿulamā* could not accept that, so they tried a third time and the third time the turban came to that one. Then they heard a voice coming from Sayyīdīna ʿUbaydullāh al-Ahrār's room, saying, "This is my *khalīfah,* follow him!"

No one had ever given that chosen *khalīfah* any attention. *Awlīyāullāh* are like that: they don't show themselves. He was at the door cleaning the shoes. Do you see anyone here cleaning the shoes? There are some who think like Pharoah when he commanded Mūsā ﷺ, *Anā rabbukumu'l-ʿalā,* "I am your Most High Lord!" They think they have access here and there, but actually they forced or imposed themselves here and there, up and down, thinking they are the godfather (overlord) of this house, of this *maqām,* or of this mosque. They are nothing! They are less than ants! It might be someone came here, sat patiently for one year and did not see Mawlana Shaykh is better than someone sitting with Mawlana Shaykh daily!

O people, don't think that one sitting with Mawlana is (spiritually) near to the shaykh, no! They are forcing themselves to be in the shaykh's place and the shaykh is not saying any word because he is submitting to Allāh's will. He accepts everything Allāh ﷻ sends. He doesn't say, "This one comes in and not this one." As we said, *Allāhu yumhil wa lā yuhmil,* "Allāh ﷻ will give you time, but He will never leave you. He will punish you at the end."

Murshid at-Tarbīyyah, like Sulṭān al-Awlīyā, *Sayyīdī* Shaykh Muhammad Nazim al-Haqqani ق, has the power to know what trust you accepted in the presence of Allāh ﷻ at that time of *alastu bī rabbikūm qālū bala,* when Allāh ﷻ asked all souls, "Am I not your Lord?" and we answered, "Yes." What kind of trust we have accepted? When you say yes, you are a servant to Allāh ﷻ, you have accepted what Allāh gave you.

What did He give you, do you know? We don't know because we are blind! We did not achieve the level of beginner yet. Don't say you have been in *ṭarīqah* a long time; to become even a beginner is so difficult!

All those that represent Mawlana Shaykh Nazim, with complete respect to them, they are not even beginners yet; they are still at the level of lovers and their love is according to what is in their hearts. Some love Mawlana so they will be famous or respected; some love Mawlana to take the money and put it in their pockets. You must know who is that one you are dealing with, and if you can't figure it out, Allāh knows who is that one!

For example, these guests visiting here are from Spain. They come out of love for Mawlana Shaykh. They are poor, yet spent their hard-earned money for tickets that costs at least five-hundred Euros plus expenses of their group. They come and wait, wait, wait, wait, wait. Finally they see Mawlana for two minutes and they are so happy, they go back home. They did not come for *dunyā*, for business, but only from love to Mawlana Shaykh. Italians, Argentineans, Americans, British, Europeans, Malaysians, Indonesians, Africans, Arabs... they come from all over the world from their love to Mawlana Shaykh and yet there are doorkeepers who block them from seeing their shaykh!

They claim they are running Mawlana's affairs, but *awlīyāullāh* don't need anyone to run their affairs, angels and *mu'min jinn* run their affairs! They run the affairs of the whole world, so they cannot support *awlīyāullāh*? Who can claim they are running the affairs of the shaykh? The shaykh doesn't need that from anyone, and there are so many who are happy to serve him simply and purely from their love, but they are blocked. Anyone coming here likes to serve their shaykh!

A simple question is, who runs your affairs: the shaykh or you? (The shaykh.) Do you run his affairs? (Never!) Those who are hearing this, don't claim to run Mawlana's affairs! Repent to Allāh ﷻ; the door is still open for you to repent. But also you must apologize to those whom you injured. Allāh ﷻ will accept your repentance as he is The Forgiver, Who forgives everyone who sincerely turns to Him.

As an example of who is running affairs of the shaykh, Grandshaykh ق and Mawlana Shaykh Nazim said here in their notes, that *walī*, the Murshid at-Tarbīyyah, knows everything about what you committed to do in Allāh's Divine Presence on the Day of Promises. He knows all about what you said and what you accepted in that divine gathering of human beings when Allāh ﷻ gave you your trust. Everyone took a trust, everyone knows what his trust is, and no two trusts are the same. Furthermore, in the Naqshbandi Order, a *walī* cannot be a *walī*, a Sulṭānu 'l-Awlīyā cannot be a Sulṭānu 'l-Awlīyā without knowing the trust of not only his *murīds* but of everyone on Earth! He must know fully, what is that trust and how can he run their affairs and help them. So, who is helping who?

Murshid at-Tarbīyyah knows everyone's affairs, everyone's trusts, including those who passed away and those who are living in his time! He knows by their name every individual Allāh ﷻ created, because he is inheriting from Adam ؑ the secret of:

*Wa 'allama Adama al-asmā kullahā.*
*And He taught Adam all the names (of everything).*
*Surātu 'l-Baqara (The Cow), 2:31*

It means He taught Adam ؑ the names of all human beings, animals, trees, even worms; everything ever created. Don't think a leaf of a tree has no name; no leaf will drop without Allāh ﷻ's permission. That's not simple in *ṭarīqah,* that is huge. Every leaf of every tree, with thousands of leaves on one tree and countless leaves in the forest, each leaf has a name. Don't think it's too much for Allāh ﷻ as His greatness will never end!

Grandshaykh ق said, "From the day Allāh ﷻ created Sayyīdīna Adam ﷺ and Adam came on Earth and Allāh created from Adam children, until the Day of Judgment, Murshid at-Tarbīyyah knows all their names. And not only their names, he has to know them one by one, what they are doing, how they are living, how long they will live, and how many breaths they will breathe before they die. And he must know their genealogy to Adam ﷺ."

These are the characteristics we have touched on today, the highest levels of guidance of Murshid at-Tarbīyyah.

## The Wisdom of Saints and Idiocy of Their Followers

By the order of Mawlana Shaykh Muhammad Nazim Adil al-Haqqani, I am speaking to you. If he did not order me I would not speak, because I took an oath a long time ago that I will not speak in this *dargah,* because we are all followers of Mawlana Shaykh and some people might think, "Why this one is speaking and not me?" So it is better not to say anything; I would rather keep quiet, as it is easier and less problematic. *Alḥamdūlillāh,* all of us are swimming in Mawlana's ocean!

*Awlīyāullāh* have a wisdom in every movement, and Grandshaykh (may Allāh bless his soul) and Mawlana Shaykh Nazim (may Allāh give him long life) said, "Our discipline is that when the shaykh is giving *ṣuḥbah,* the *murīd* must always be attentive. He must not move his eyes from looking near the shaykh, he must tune his ears to what the shaykh is speaking, and he must write notes." That is because when you write you can memorize and retain it easier, but when it is recorded you will not.

Grandshaykh ق said, "If someone so much as scratches his face when the shaykh is speaking, it will bring the association down seven levels." It means we have to be well-disciplined, not moving. We must be like the trained guards you see in front of castles or palaces, not distracted by anyone or anything for even a moment. He said when they are sitting and someone comes from the door, many people attending the *ṣuḥbah* look at that one, which is *tarku 'l-adab,* losing your discipline in the presence of the shaykh. To look at others is not your business; your business is with the shaykh. You must not look outside; you have to look within yourself, where the problem is. We have to look inward, not outward. When we look outwardly, we will be exhausted as the problems never end. First we must fix ourselves.

So imagine, in the presence of the Prophet ﷺ, do you think a *walī* has time to scratch his ears or his head? No way. If you are in the presence of a VIP, an important personality, would you do that? Or would you change your way of sitting this way or that way, or would you keep perfectly still? The *adab* is to not move. So what about sitting with a *walī*? Do we sit like that? No. What about being in the holy presence of Prophet ﷺ? What about in Allāh's Divine Presence?

Prophet ﷺ said, when we enter the prayer we are in the Divine Presence praying in front of Allāh ﷻ. Although you are not seeing that, you will be there. That is why our eyes must remain on where we make *sajdah,* where we prostrate. It is extremely bad *adab* for our eyes to wander in *ṣalāt*. We must discipline ourselves to look inward and focus on what we are doing to understand *awlīyāullāh*. Otherwise, if we focus externally we might fall into the trap of gossip and lose everything and waste our energy.

Murshid at-Tarbīyyah knows what trust we took from Allāh ﷻ. We do not know because our bad manners and bad characters veil our hearts. Murshid at-Tarbīyyah knows because Allāh gave him the ability to raise Ummati Muhammad ﷺ, so they know about your past, present and future, all the way back to Adam ﷺ and all the way forward to the Day of Judgment. They know about your ancestors, your descendants, to whom you are related, and what trust you received. They clean you and present you daily to Prophet ﷺ.

Murshid at-Tarbīyyah can look on the Preserved Tablets and see precisely what is written for every living servant of Allāh ﷻ, and what each person has to do according to the trust he was given. He is able to confirm what Allāh ﷻ changes on the Preserved Tablets and guides you through inspirations to your heart by permission of Prophet ﷺ. He guides you daily through your heart when you are reflecting your thoughts on the shaykh, and from the shaykh to Prophet ﷺ, and from Prophet to Allāh ﷻ. That gives you a *wasīlah,* advice or instructions, on how to move forward quickly like a rocket. They take you and move you from one side to another side. So meditation and contemplation are very important in Islam, as Prophet ﷺ said in the *Ḥadīth Qudsī*:

*Tafakkaru saʿatin khayrun min ʿibādati sabaʿīn sannah.*
*To contemplate Allāh's Greatness and Prophet's mercy and the shaykh's love, you will be rewarded the worship of 70 years.*

As we mentioned before, Murshid at-Taṣfīyyah (the third level) is able to look between the two breaths of *murīds* he is responsible for, breathing in and breathing out. Between these two breaths there are 24,000 wisdoms, and he can reach up to 12,000 wisdoms. But Murshid at-Tarbīyyah can reach the 24,000 wisdoms; he sees them and can throw them into your heart. On the Day of Judgment you will be raised as if during your journey you learned these 24,000 wisdoms given to you in every inhalation and exhalation! On the Day of Judgment, you will appear with that *ʿibādah* in the presence of Prophet ﷺ and in the Divine Presence of Allāh ﷻ.

Also, Allāh ﷻ gives every human being different wisdom than others, because your trust is different from anyone else's trust. Those unique wisdoms Allāh ﷻ bestows are covered, and you cannot get them if you are not reaching high levels of servant hood. So Murshid at-Tarbīyyah keeps this trust for you until you die or until the Day of Judgment.

So let's calculate our daily breaths. If a cycle of inhalation and exhalation take 5 seconds, it means every minute we take an average of 12 breaths, every hour we 720 breaths, and every 24 hours we take 17,280 breaths. Multiply that by 24,000 wisdoms Allāh ﷻ is giving you everyday and it becomes millions! Your shaykh is carrying that trust for you. If you reach the required spiritual level, he delivers it to you in *dunyā*. If not, he won't give you diamonds when you don't appreciate them, but he will give you candies to keep you around, to maintain your love for him, which is okay. Your trust cannot be delivered until you are reaching the highest level of your journey.

Murshid at-Tarbīyyah keeps that for you and in every 24 hours during Ṣalātu 'n-Najāt he uploads that to your heart. To access it you need a code that is only granted when the shaykh presents you clean with this *ibādah* to Prophet ﷺ. Although this is beyond our mind's limitations, don't think *awlīyāullāh* have nothing to do! Even this is an inaccurate description, a limitation of their heavenly powers which our minds cannot grasp.

May Allāh ﷻ give our shaykh long life! We must know we are fortunate and honored to be connected to him because he has all these characteristics and powers, but he shows some and he hides many. He is not going to give everything. He gives some drops, crumbs, a little bit to enjoy, but this is enough for us because we cannot carry more. If this lamp is wired for 110 volts of electricity and you give it 220 volts, it will explode. *Awlīyāullāh* will not give you more than you can carry. Our light is a dim nightlight; a small light in the corner of the room, but it is a light.

We must be happy, because every one of you is a light. Mawlana is proud of his students because they are delivering his message, something from the love of your shaykh, presenting and explaining about your shaykh's greatness and knowledge, his honor and blessing. So it means everyone has a position.

One time Mawlana Shaykh told me, "Hisham Effendi, all of them are like diamonds on my turban, and every diamond represents one of them. If that diamond is broken, my turban, my crown is broken because it looks bad." Human nature is to see the negative, so in a museum when you see a crown on display, if any place on that crown is missing jewels, your eye will notice it immediately. Then you don't think, "Oh *mashā'Allāh*, this crown is so beautiful," you think, "What is so great about this crown with missing jewels?" *Murīds* are diamonds on their shaykh's turban; that is how high the shaykh regards you! The diamonds are those who come to the shaykh with no intention of getting anything, only coming for the love of their shaykh. For those who come for worldly benefit—and there are many—Mawlana Shaykh says, "Take *dunyā*, I don't care!"

I will tell you a nice story that explains this. Ten years ago in America, a lady telephoned from England insisting to speak with me. I didn't know her. She called the office daily for a week and they transferred the line, saying it's an emergency.

She said, "I cannot say this to you; I have to meet Mawlana Shaykh Nazim immediately. Every day I stand waiting to meet Mawlana in a long queue, and he cannot see everyone and says, 'Come tomorrow.' This is a life or death situation!"

So to help her, I called Mawlana on the phone and said, "Please Mawlana, this lady is saying this and it is very urgent."

Mawlana Shaykh said, "Okay. Send her to me tomorrow and tell her to mention her name; even if the line is long I will know her name and they will bring her in."

So when she arrived, and again the queue was so long, she said, "I have an appointment."

They said, "Here there is no appointment, you stand in line like everyone else."

She said, "I am so-and-so. Shaykh Hisham arranged for me; please let me in to see Mawlana Shaykh.".

They said, "Oh! Okay. Mawlana is waiting for you."

Mawlana Shaykh put her inside because she said it was a matter of life or death. She came in and Mawlana said, "What is the problem?"

She said, "O my master, I have a big problem! I am renovating my house and everything is finished except the kitchen. I need to know what color to paint it! I am calling and calling for this reason."

Mawlana said, "For this you are coming here? Paint it any color you like!

She insisted, "No Mawlana, pick a color for me!"

Mawlana looked at her and said, "Call Shaykh Hisham."

They called me and Mawlana was not happy, saying, "What are you are sending to me?"

So there are people who come to the shaykh to waste his time with petty *dunyā* matters. Ask him, "What heavenly paint do I need for my soul, O my teacher!" don't come for *dunyā, dunyā, dunyā, dunyā, dunyā* problems; it will not benefit you. You can ask Mawlana Shaykh, "*Yā* Sayyidi, pray for me."

Allāh ﷻ does not look at your faces, your colors, at your outward appearances; He looks at your hearts. If your heart is good, you are good. If your heart is not good, you are not good. So when *awlīyāullāh* look at the Preserved Tablets, they see everyone's heart is clean, because according to the *Ḥadīth Qudsī* of Prophet ﷺ, every human being is born on innocence as Allāh created us pure; either his parents make him Jewish, following the Jewish belief, or make him Christian, following the Christian belief, or at that time Zoroastrian, following the Zoroastrian belief.

Why didn't Prophet ﷺ mention Islam? It means human beings are already created as Muslims, as Sayyīdīnā 'Ibrāhīm ﷺ said, *Yā Rabbī* I am Muslim; I am not *mushrik* (polytheist). From him came all religions, so the beginning of religions was Islam. So every human being is born on Islam and thus the *ḥadīth* does not mention it. Your origin is Islam, which means the light of that faith is inside and no one can put it down. When Allāh ﷻ gives something, no one can take it. Even if you become a different religion if you are not Muslim, if you are Jewish or Christian or Buddhist or whatever, it's like a garment you can change at any time and turn back to your origin.

Why do deceased people go to the grave naked? In Islam we are wrapped in a shroud of unstitched cloth before entering the grave. We don't dress in a suit and tie, because we came to *dunyā* and when we die, Allāh ﷻ dresses us in heavenly clothes, which is Islam.

*Verily, the religion with Allāh is Islam.*

*Sūrat Ālī-'Imrān (The Family of Imrān), 3:19*

*Awlīyāullāh* see in the Preserved Tablets what you will wear in *dunyā* of wild and good characters. Prophet ﷺ said, "I observe the *'amal* of my *Ummah*. If I find good, I pray for them." Everyday Prophet ﷺ sees what you do. If you are doing good deeds he is happy, he praises Allāh ﷻ, and prays for you. If he sees something bad, he asks Allāh ﷻ to forgive you.

*Awlīyāullāh* inherit that secret from Prophet ﷺ, to see on the Preserved Tablets what their followers are doing, good or bad. If they are doing good deeds, *awlīyāullāh* are happy, and if they are doing bad deeds, they clean them and present them to Prophet ﷺ.

Who can stand up and say they have this power? So all representatives of Mawlana Shaykh around the world, don't claim something that doesn't belong to you! If you have that character, come in front of us, claim it, and say, "Yes, we are like that."

May Allāh guide us and guide them, protect us and protect them, and give us the *barakah* of this day and everyday. May Allāh take away from us all bad *'amal* and replace them with good *'amal*. We are asking, *yā Rabbī*, who hurt us we are forgiving them in *dunyā*, but not in *Ākhirah*. In *Ākhirah* we need our rights from them! Although it is good to say, "I am forgiving him in *dunyā* and *Ākhirah*," is it not? It is even better to say, "May Allāh forgive them in *dunyā* and *Ākhirah*."

*Lā yuḥibbu 'Llāhu 'l-jahra bi 's-sūi mina 'l-qawli illa man ẓulima wa kāna Allāhu samī'an 'alīma.*

*Allāh loves not that evil should be voiced in public except where injustice has been done, for Allah is All-Hearing and All-Knowing.* *Sūratu 'n-Nisā (The Women), 4:148*

*wa lahu mā sakana fī 'l-layli wa an-nahāri wa huwa as-samīʿu 'l-ʿalim.*
*And to Him belongs whatever exists in the night and the day, and He is the All-Hearing, the All-Knowing."*
*Sūratu 'l-`Anʿām (The Cattle), 6:13*

By Allāh's order, if you are oppressed you have the fundamental right to expose your oppressor. Allāh is as-Samī', The All-Hearing (of all things in the past, the present and in the future). He hears those who backbite you and throw confusion and spread rumors. He is al-ʿAlīm, The All-Knowing, and He will punish those who injured you and restore your rights.

So we say, "*Yā Rabbī,* we forgive them in *dunyā* and *Ākhirah,* but we need our rights from them in *Ākhirah.*" If they don't apologize in *dunyā,* never mind, we want them to apologize in *Ākhirah,* which is going to be very difficult. In *dunyā* you say, "*As-salāmu ʿalaykum,* I'm sorry. Thank you," and it's resolved. But in *Ākhirah,* you take all of their *ḥasanāt,* so we are going to take it there, *inshāAllāh*!

They closed Peckham Mosque, they closed Shacklewell Lane Mosque, they closed Green Lanes mosque, they closed St. Anne's Priory, all for business! It's not simple; mosques are for Allāh ﷻ, so it is not their property, they are squatters! They went in and changed everything and refuse to leave, saying, "You owe us money." In January 2009, Mawlana Shaykh recorded his declaration for United Kingdom that he doesn't like mosques to be used for collecting money. They are not only collecting every Friday, they are renting the place!

May Allāh forgive us and them. May Allāh ﷻ change our hearts and their hearts to love of Prophet ﷺ and love of Mawlana Shaykh.

## Ways of Moral Excellence

Allāh ﷻ said in Holy Qur'an:

> *O you who believe! Enter not houses other than your own, until you have asked permission and greeted those in them; that is better for you, in order that you may remember.*
>
> *Sūratu n-Nūr (The Light), 24:27*

In Islam there is guidance for entering a house, and it is unacceptable to enter from the windows. You must show respect by approaching the proper door, knocking, and waiting for permission to enter. If the door is already open you may enter, but if the door is not open you cannot enter. Allāh revealed in Holy Qur'an that people came to the house of Prophet ﷺ to consult him when he is sitting with his family, and it was hurting the Prophet ﷺ.

So we learn from this that there is a way of respect for all things. Even if you want to give an advice or to speak, there must be a way of respect, and that is to have permission. You cannot speak without permission. When you speak without permission that light is not there, but only a negative reflection will come to the heart of the listeners instead of a positive reflection. When you have permission, that light will come with it, to who is speaking and to who is listening. That's why it is necessary to have the right permission from the right person. Then it will not be your speech, it will be his speech, as he is responsible by giving you permission to speak. Mawlana Shaykh ق told me to speak; I am speaking and he is telling us to listen, and all of us benefit from the light coming on us.

As I narrated previously, when Sayyīdīnā Shaykh Sharafuddīn ق passed away Grandshaykh 'AbdAllāh al-Fā'iz ad-Dāghestānī tore his will and threw it in the river because he didn't want anyone to know he is a *walī* and the successor of Shaykh Sharafuddīn. This the way of *awlīyāullāh:* although they already tamed their ego, still they want to put more and more pressure on their ego so it will not play with them, so they hide themselves. This is a characteristic of all great *awlīyā* such as Sulṭān al-Awlīyā, Mawlana Shaykh Nazim, may Allāh ﷻ grant him long life!

One week before Grandshaykh ق left *dunyā*, he wrote his will and he said, "I am leaving *dunyā* and pass my will to Mawlana Shaykh Nazim." That was 4th of Ramadan and Mawlana Shaykh Nazim was in Cyprus. As we were so much in love with Grandshaykh, we said, "Oh no way Grandshaykh will die!" Out of love you can imagine everything and you can say whatever you want to say. That's why when Prophet ﷺ left *dunyā*, Sayyīdīnā 'Umar ؓ said, "If anyone says that Prophet died I will cut his neck!" He could not bring himself to believe that news, until Sayyīdīnā Abū Bakr ق recited the verse of Holy Qur'an:

> *Muhammad is no more than a messenger, and indeed messengers have passed away before him. If he dies or is killed, will you then turn back on your heels (as unbelievers)? And he who turns back on his heels, not the least harm will he do to Allāh, and Allāh will give reward to those who are grateful.*
>
> *Sūrat Ālī-'Imrān (The Family of Imrān), 3:144*

It means Prophet ﷺ is going to die and he died. 'Umar kept quiet and calmed down. So out of love, anyone can do anything. You see today people commit suicide if their love did not work out. So, out of love we believed Grandshaykh will never leave *dunyā*.

One week later on Sunday, Grandshaykh ق was laying in his bed attended to by two doctors, my brother and another doctor, and me and Shaykh Adnan, so three brothers were there. I was sitting beside Grandshaykh, who said, "Hold my hand and count my pulse." I was not able to count it; it was more than 170 or 180. He ordered everyone— me, my brother, my other brother, the doctor, and another doctor—out of the room, to go upstairs, that he wanted to relax. We went out, and after five minutes his daughter, Hajjah Madiha, shouted, "Oh my father! Come quickly to see what is happening to my father!" We came running, but Grandshaykh, may Allāh bless his soul, had already left *dunyā*.

As a medical doctor, my brother immediately began CPR to bring him back, but it did not work. The other doctor was a cardiologist, so he went to his car to get some adrenalin to inject into Grandshaykh's heart to hopefully restart it. It took five or six minutes for him to run to the car and return, and then to prepare the injection, another two minutes. My brother took the syringe to inject the heart of Grandshaykh, who had no pulse, it was zero.

At that moment, Grandshaykh opened his eyes and sat up on his bed and said in Turkish, "Leave it! Don't touch that!" He then lay back down. We were already in shock that he had left *dunyā*, but this surprised us even more! These are the ways of *awlīyāullāh*. If you tell anyone this story they might not believe it, saying it is an exaggeration, but I saw this with my own eyes.

That night we washed Grandshaykh ق to prepare him for burial, and the next morning we wrapped him in his shroud. We were ready to go to Nabīullāh Dhul-Kifl Cemetery, named for Sayyīdīna Nabīullāh Dhul-Kifl ﷺ, which was very close to Grandshaykh's house. He bought a grave there because, as he said, "That cemetery is full of prophets." Grandshaykh has one grave there, and he ordered Mawlana Shaykh Nazim, may Allāh give him long life, me, and my brother Shaykh Adnan to have graves there: you can see our names there on those graves.

The night Grandshaykh passed away, we complied with the local formality and contacted the city to dig the grave. Afterwards we received inspiration from Mawlana Shaykh Nazim to bury Grandshaykh in his mosque. Because of that local policy, we called the grave digger to come to Grandshaykh's mosque and he said, "I already finished digging the grave in the cemetery, it's ready." We said, "But we don't want to bury him there!"

When you have permission, real inspirations come to guide you. Mawlana Shaykh Nazim was still in Cyprus and we tried to send him a message that Grandshaykh had passed away, to come quickly, but it was very difficult. Someone came 'out of the blue' (from nowhere) and said, "I can send him a message." We knew he was not able, but we said, "Send a message to Mawlana Shaykh Nazim to come."

It is a small mosque. When Grandshaykh built it he saw Prophet ﷺ telling him to build it according to the specifications of the original Kaʿaba. Grandshaykh said, "*Yā Sayyīdī, Yā Rasūlullāh*, how will I know where to build it?" Prophet ﷺ said, "Don't worry, tomorrow you will find the sign." The next day four huge nails appeared in the ground next to Grandshaykh's house on Jabal Qāsiyūn, marking the four corners of the *masjid*! Allāh ﷻ did not cover or block anything from *awlīyāullāh*. This is the characteristic of Murshid at-Tarbīyyah.

So we said to the grave digger, "Can you dig a grave here in the *masjid*." He said, "No, it's against the law, I cannot." We said, "Please, you know Grandshaykh." He said, "I cannot do that, I am sorry to say." Then we gave him some money and he said, "Of course, I can dig the grave!" and he did. He said, "But when the funeral procession comes up the hill, make sure that everyone thinks it is going to the cemetery. When you pass, don't take the road to the cemetery, turn and go toward his house, and tell people, 'From that way we are going to the cemetery.' Then come here and put him in the grave in his *masjid.*"

So, big *ʿulamā* came to Damascus, we prayed Ṣalātu 'l-Janāzah and Ṣalātu 'l-Ẓuhr. Fifty or sixty-thousand people were in the *janāzah* procession going slowly up the mountain's narrow street and it was near ʿAṣr time. We were all fasting and it was so hot, as Damascus is normally very hot in October. When we reached, we did not go to the cemetery, we went to the *masjid* and we put the coffin there. Just then someone came 'out of the blue', standing on the hill, saying, "Don't bury Grandshaykh, Shaykh Nazim is sending a message he will arrive soon."

We thought, "How he is arriving when there is no flight from Cyprus to Damascus?" At that time, once or twice a week a flight was only available into Beirut Airport.

So we said, "Okay, we will wait."

The *ʿulamā* did not want to wait, but me and my brother were young and crazy, and we stopped them, saying, "No way we are going to bury Grandshaykh, until Mawlana Shaykh Nazim arrives!"

They said, "You have to bury him."

We said, "We are not going to bury him!"

They said, "You are crazy to not bury him now! We are leaving. With whom we are going to shake hands?"

We said, "Shake hands with us and go."

So they shook our hands, saying, "May Allāh bless his soul," and they made *duʿa* and left.

ʿAṣr time came and Mawlana Shaykh did not arrive yet, and we were anxious as it was going to be night. At Maghrib we were all saying, *"Allāhu Akbar"* and Mawlana reached the bottom of the road where it comes to the *masjid*. We were very happy. He came quickly to the *masjid* and said to everyone, "I don't want anyone to stay here; go and break fast." He sent everyone out except me and my brother. We again prayed Ṣalātu 'l-Janāzah. Mawlana Shaykh Nazim entered the grave; we handed him the body, which he laid to rest with his own hands, and we covered the grave. Then he said, "You and your brother also go up to eat and close the *masjid* on me."

We closed the door but there was a window there, and we were looking to see what's going on, why everyone has to go out? We saw Mawlana Shaykh Nazim stand facing the body and he vanished! Where he went? The Earth did not open that he went down, and the roof did not open for him to go out! We decided to go in, that maybe we would disappear with him, but we were shaking to open the door. So, we kept looking from the window and about ten minutes later, suddenly he reappeared.

Mawlana Shaykh opened the door and we said, "Mawlana, there is no way we can go eat now, until you tell us what just happened!"

He said, "That is not for you."

We said, "For us or not for us, we don't know. But you have to tell us what happened!"

He said, "Come inside."

We went inside and Mawlana Shaykh said, "As soon as I stood up and you saw me give respect, that moment Sayyīdīnā Muhammad ﷺ appeared with all prophets, with Mahdī ؑ and all his *khulafā* and deputies and ministers, and *awlīyāullāh*. They took Mawlana's body all the way to Madīnatu 'l-Munawwarah, so I went with that procession. They welcomed him in Madinah in the presence of Prophet ﷺ, and they brought him back because he is *barakah* for all Shām (Damascus), because Sham is going to be the Throne of Allāh

ﷻ, as Prophet ﷺ mentioned. Prophets and *awlīyā* have been moved to Sham, so they brought him back."

This story is better than everything we were discussing!

When *awlīyāullāh* receive permission, they have such high discipline and Allāh ﷻ gives them everything. Discipline is important. When people have no respect, no discipline toward each other, never their hearts will open for spirituality. Spirituality cannot come to a dirty heart, it can only come to a clean heart. You cannot pray on a rug that it is dirty, but you can clean it with water and then you can pray on it because it became pure. It's like that with spirituality: you can clean yourself with a shower or an ablution and then you can have a clean heart. It means you can repent at any time and Allāh ﷻ will forgive you. That's no problem, but we have to remember to repent.!

Let's go back to the original story. Grandshaykh said to us, "Pass this will to Mawlana Shaykh Nazim." In his will, the first page contained all the instructions for physical inheritance, who will inherit what from him, 'to whom, to whom, to whom.' The second page contained his instructions for the spiritual inheritance. Grandshaykh wrote, "After me, by order of Prophet ﷺ, I have ordered my son, Nazim Effendi, for many, many seclusions to prepare him to carry that responsibility of secrets that I was carrying from my shaykh all the way to Prophet ﷺ. I am passing that secret to him, and I gave two helpers, you and your brother, to be with him always, helping him whenever he needs and to be in different places."

*InshāAllāh* Tomorrow I will tell you how that secret was passed to him and what we witnessed. What we did not see might be more, but I can speak about what I saw.

Me and my brother were very honored for our names to have been included there. We never expected or asked for that, and we never knew it would happen, except what we saw in that will.

That night after we buried Grandshaykh, we went to break fast and Mawlana Shaykh Nazim ate very little and we did not eat. We came to his house and gave him the will. He was sad and said, "I don't want to see it now." After losing the most precious one in your life, do you want to see the will? He was not looking for that. Today when people lose their father or mother they don't care, they want to see the will immediately, to know what they will inherit.

Three days of mourning passed, which is *sunnah*. Mawlana Shaykh said, "First let's go to Beirut, and from Beirut I am going to Cyprus."

We asked again, "Do you want to see the will?"

"No."

So we came to Beirut and Mawlana said he will see the will. He read it, kissed it, put it on his head, and said, "Put it in a safe-box." We had an old, huge safe-box (*sandūq*) that no one can move, and no one can open it without the set of three keys. We put the will in it.

Mawlana Shaykh stayed another two days to get the flight and before leaving he said, "Get me the will; I will kiss it another time. You put it in the safe-box."

We opened the safe-box and the will had disappeared! It was one of two; one copy Grandshaykh ordered us to put in his grave, because he wanted to go to Allāh ﷻ with the will in his hand showing to whom he delivered the secret, while he is leaving *dunyā* with nothing else to give. The second copy stayed with us. From that copy we made a copy of the main page, and we never thought to copy the second page about the spiritual inheritance!

So, this is an example of how *awlīyāullāh* don't want to show themselves. Mawlana Shaykh Nazim didn't want to carry or display the will anywhere. He didn't want anyone to know who is he, and he left. At that time, there were five representatives of Grandshaykh: Mawlana Shaykh, Sulṭān al-Awlīyā *Sayyīdī* Shaykh Muhammad Nazim al-Haqqani ق, Shaykh Ḥusayn ق, Shaykh Aḥmad Nidami ق, Abū Hisham ق, and there is one more. Only Shaykh Ḥusayn accepted Shaykh Nazim as Mawlana Shaykh's successor; everyone went their own way and made another branch. Like in the time of Shaykh Sharafuddīn ق, no one followed Grandshaykh as his successor, they made their own branches, and that's why the secret is not known. Everyone thought Grandshaykh ق was just a normal person. They called him "Hajji ʿAbdAllāh"; that's what they knew of him as he hid the will.

Although Mawlana Shaykh Nazim hid the will, when it was written there were six or seven witnesses who all knew what is in it, but they didn't support that. In any case, in 1974, Mawlana Shaykh Nazim was ordered, he received permission, to move *ṭarīqah* to Europe, and Allāh ﷻ opened east and west to him! Today you see such diversity among the people coming to him now. From every part of the world Allāh ﷻ is sending them, to show that he is Sulṭān al-Awlīyā, as the *sulṭān* receives from everywhere in beautiful colors like a rainbow.

May Allāh ﷻ keep that rainbow of Sulṭān al-Awlīyā to continuously shine on us!

## How the Secret Was Passed to Mawlana Shaykh

I promised to tell you how that secret was transferred to Mawlana Shaykh Nazim. There are twenty-eight letters are in the Arabic language, and an extra one is the letter *"Lā"* (*lām alīf*), so there are twenty-nine letters. According to *ʿulamā* and *awlīyāullāh*, every letter is one *manzil* of the light reflected by the moon, which appears and disappears within twenty-nine days. So every day the appearance of the moon is describing one letter of the Arabic alphabet, what we call a *manzil.*

It is well-known and established in science that the moon's reflection greatly influences the character of human beings in various ways. That is because the moon has a special kind of gravity which is lighter than the Earth. Because of the reflection of the moon we have high and low tides on Earth, and people experience various affections. But why? Prophet ﷺ described moonlight as the sun's reflection.

Prophet ﷺ represents the moon, as he is "Sirājān Munīrāh."

> *wa dāʿīan ila-Llāhi bi idhnihi wa Sirājān Munīrāh.*
> *And as one who invites unto Allāh by His permission, and as a lamp that gives light."* *Sūratu'l-Aḥzāb (The Groups), 33:46*

> *...qad jā'akum mina 'Llāhi nūrun wa kitābun mubīn.*
> *There has come to you from Allāh a (new) light and a perspicuous Book.* *Sūratu 'l-Mā'idah (The Table Spread), 5:15*

Muslim scholars agree, that new light, *nūr,* is Muhammad ﷺ. So in the symbolism of a human being, what does the moon represent and what is the sun? The moon of each human being is the heart. The body is a piece of flesh. The moon, *qamar,* is a piece of a planet with no life on it. The heart too, is a piece of flesh. What makes the heart function? It is the *rūḥ,* spirit. Thus the heart of the human being is described as the moon and the *rūḥ* is described as the sun, the source of its energy and life.

When you are able to make the *rūḥ* dominate the heart, then you will become a reflector of light. At that time the heart begins to reflect light and knowledge. When you cause the heart to dominate the *rūḥ* by covering it with the worldly life, that *rūḥ* is compressed and repressed so it can no longer appear. Under the pressure of bad desires, the heart's light fades.

Thus, the heart is the seat of good desires and bad desires. If one allows the bad desires to control the heart, the light of the heart is extinguished, the fountain of knowledge stops flowing, and one becomes attached to *dunyā*.

When you put down evil desires of the heart and promote the *rūḥ*, then just as the sun dominates the entire sky when it appears, so too will every cell of your body begin reflecting light to humanity. That is how the Sahaba ﷺ were able to attract masses of people around the world, because they were speaking in the form of *rūḥ*. That light which they take from the main source of energy and reflect through their bodies is enough to change the hearts of people immediately!

> *Yā ayyuha 'n-nabīyyu innā arsalnāka shāhidan wa mubash-shiran wa nadhīra.*
> *O Prophet! Verily, We have sent you as witness, and a bearer of glad tidings, and a warner. Sūratu'l-Aḥzāb (The Groups), 33:45*

Sayyīdīna Muhammad ﷺ was sent by Allāh ﷻ as His messenger, to give glad tidings from Allāh, to warn people of danger, and to call people to Allāh. He is Sirājān Munīrāh, "a shining lamp (the moon)," reflecting light of the Divine Presence on all humanity. So the reflections human beings get from the moon are the lights reflected by Prophet ﷺ that affect human beings.

In our explanation of the *manzil*, every letter of the Arabic alphabet represents one portion of the knowledge that Prophet ﷺ gave to *awlīyāullāh*. There are twenty-nine letters and twenty-nine portions are being given to *awlīyāullāh*, who can take one portion from one letter. Another *walī* can take one portion from another letter, and in every letter there are infinite portions.

Grandshaykh ق said that Murshid at-Tarbīyyah, the guide at the highest level of *irshād*, must have portions of knowledge from within each letter. As Prophet ﷺ ascends and receives more knowledge, *awlīyāullāh* also receive more knowledge from him; he ﷺ gives to them continuously, so they receive knowledge from him in one ascension, then in another ascension.

He ﷺ will even give them knowledge from the same letter, different portions with different knowledges. Whenever Prophet ﷺ gives to *awlīyāullāh*, at the same time it appears on the Preserved Tablets. Grandshaykh ق said Murshid at-Tarbīyyah must have all the knowledge of the alphabet which also appears on the Preserved Tablets; he has full access.

Some institutions or governments restrict access to crucial details and make it "classified information." Murshid at-Tarbīyyah has access to all classified information. Prophet ﷺ gives to various *awlīyāullāh*, whereas they do not, because they have only one portion of one *manzil*. That may be simple to explain in words, but through genuine experience, in reality this is above our limited understanding.

Such knowledge cannot be given by books, papers, by writing, or by professors or scholars through their presentations; it is only conveyed from heart to heart. You cannot give it in a different way, as explained in the story of Sayyīdīnā Aḥmad al-Badawī ق, how that *walī* met him, took his knowledge from him, and filled him with another kind of knowledge poured into his heart.

That's why it is said in a well-known *ḥadīth* that what Allāh ﷻ gave to Prophet ﷺ, Prophet ﷺ gave to Sayyīdīnā Abū Bakr ق in his heart.

> *Whatever Allāh poured into my heart, I poured into the heart of Abū Bakr.* *Sahih Bukhārī*

He used the word *ṣabba*, meaning "poured." This is not like when Abū Hurayrah ؓ said, "I have memorized from Prophet ﷺ two kinds of knowledges: one kind I share with everyone and the other kind, if I share it they will cut my neck." It means other Ṣaḥābah ؓ might object to what he would reveal of hidden knowledge from Prophet ﷺ. Abū Hurayrah ؓ received a lot of *aḥadīth* from Prophet ﷺ that was not shared with anyone else. Others learned different *aḥadīth*. Abū Hurayrah ؓ revealed it in that *ḥadīth* without seeing what it is.

Today some scholars say, "Oh no, it's about the signs of the Last Days". But signs of the Last Days are already mentioned there in books of *ḥadīth*. You can find it in any of the collections of *ḥadīth*. But we don't know what he hid from the other Ṣaḥābah. That is the heavenly knowledge that Prophet ﷺ gave.

Even Sayyīdīna Abū Bakr aṣ-Ṣiddīq ق narrated approximately twenty *aḥadīth* (few), and he is the *ṣāḥib*[18] of Rasūlullāh ﷺ, whom Allāh ﷻ mentioned in Holy Qur'an.

This is a story from Grandshaykh's hidden knowledges:

When Prophet ﷺ and Abū Bakr aṣ-Ṣiddīq ق hid in the cave during *hijrah* from Mecca to Madinah, Prophet ﷺ became tired, rested his head on the leg of Sayyīdīna Abū Bakr aṣ-Ṣiddīq ق, and fell asleep. Suddenly, tears streamed down Abū Bakr aṣ-Ṣiddīq's face, and although he tried not to disturb Prophet ﷺ, the tears fell on his holy face, awaking Prophet ﷺ. This *āyah* was revealed to him at that moment:

> *If you help (Muḥammad) not (it does not matter), for Allāh did indeed help him when the disbelievers drove him out, the second of two, when they were in the cave. And he said to his companion, "Be not sad (or afraid), surely Allāh is with us."*

---

[18] Personal friend; root of "Ṣaḥābah."

*Then Allāh sent down His Sakīnah (tranquility) upon him, and strengthened him with forces which you saw not, and made the word of those who disbelieved the lowermost, while it was the Word of Allāh that became the uppermost. And Allāh is All-Mighty, All-Wise.* *Sūratu 't-Tawba (The Repentance), 9:40*

Prophet ﷺ then said to his *ṣāḥib*, his loyal friend, "Don't be sad or afraid, for Allāh ﷻ is with us."

Grandshaykh, may Allāh bless his soul, said when they entered and Prophet ﷺ rested on Abū Bakr aṣ-Ṣiddīq's leg, there was a hole in the cave that Abū Bakr extended his feet to close as he was worried something would come out. In fact there was a snake in the cave that wanted to see Raḥmatan li 'l-'Alamīn, Sayyīdīna Muhammad ﷺ. So it bit Abū Bakr aṣ-Ṣiddīq's foot, and continued to bite, bite, bite, until it reached his knees. He was worried the snake would touch the Prophet ﷺ and began to cry. *SubḥānAllāh*! Snake bites on the feet are very painful; victims often die of a heart attack from their fear. Abū Bakr aṣ-Ṣiddīq ق was able to carry the pain of snake bites, but not the pain of potential harm to Prophet ﷺ!

As narrated by Grandshaykh ق, Abū Bakr said, "*Yā Sayyīdī, Yā Rasūlullāh!* I'm worried this snake biting my leg will come to you!"

Prophet ﷺ then spoke to the snake, "Don't you know the flesh of a *ṣiddīq* is forbidden for you to eat?"

The snake pulled back and said, "*Yā Rasūlullāh*! I did not eat it, I was only extracting and moving forward because he closed the hole. When we knew about your appearance in *dunyā*, I was so in love with you when your name was being mentioned that I was not able to hold myself! I repeatedly prayed, '*Yā Rabbī*! Give me long life to see the face of the Seal of Messengers ﷺ, the one whose name you raised with Yours!'

When you entered this cave, Abū Bakr's ق leg blocked my way. I was only biting it to get out of the hole and behold you."

Prophet ﷺ said, "Okay, you have permission."

Grandshaykh ق said the snake was coming out of the hole and turning, turning, turning, turning, turning, becoming huge and looking at Prophet ﷺ.

Prophet ﷺ said, "Look at me now."

The snake looked, was satisfied, and said, "Now your promise has been fulfilled!"

At that moment Allāh ordered the soul of the snake taken away and the snake died. Immediately, the sulṭān of *jinn* appeared, carried that snake, and threw it in the valley of Yajūj and Majūj (Gog and Magog).

When you love those with knowledge, they pour heavenly knowledge into your heart. From the knowledge poured into Abū Bakr aṣ-Ṣiddīq's heart, he mentioned approximately twenty *āḥadīth,* but where are the others? He was the closest friend of Prophet ﷺ. Abū Hurayrah ؓ mentioned around 3,000 *ḥadīth.* Where are Sayyīdīnā Abū Bakr aṣ-Ṣiddīq's ؓ *ḥadīth*? He received mostly private knowledge, and he didn't want to show any egoism so he didn't express it to anyone, he hid it.

Grandshaykh ق came to Lebanon for the surgery in the holy month of Rajab. The hernia repair surgery was completely successful, and according to the doctors the eye surgery was also successful. But afterwards, Grandshaykh stopped eating. Why? We don't know. He said he was in a complete seclusion. So we informed Mawlana Shaykh ق.

He arrived in Beirut, and was very tired. He entered the hospital room of Grandshaykh and at that moment, Mawlana Shaykh began to have pain. My brother is a surgeon, and he discovered Mawlana Shaykh had the same kind of hernia! That is the station of Fanā'un fi 'l-Mashaykh, Annihilation in the Shaykhs. If I am annihilated in you, I feel whatever happens to you and you feel whatever happens to me.

That is the highest level after Maḥabbatullah (Love of Allāh), Maḥabbatu'l-Ḥabīb (Love of Prophet), and Maḥabbatu'l-Mashaykh (Love of the Shaykhs). Then you establish presence: Ḥuḍūrullah (Presence of Allāh), Ḥuḍūru'l-Ḥabīb (Presence of Prophet), and Ḥuḍūru'l-Mashaykh (Presence of the Shaykhs). Then you establish Fanā'un fillāh (Annihilation in Allāh's Divine Presence), Fanā'un fi 'l-Ḥabīb (Annihilation in Prophet), and Fanā'un fi 'l-Mashaykh (Annihilation in the Shaykhs). The state of Fanā'un fillāh is to be in the Divine Presence, not in Allāh ﷻ Himself; there is no way for that and to think it is out of Islam.

They performed surgery on Mawlana Shaykh immediately, and they recovered side by side. Mawlana Shaykh healed quickly, as did Grandshaykh ق, but he still had the problem with his eyes. He said, "I want to speak privately with Nazim Effendi," so everyone left the room.

My brother and I were young and naughty in the Naqshbandi-Sufi Way. My brother owned that hospital and put Grandshaykh in a nice room with high ceilings, high windows and a balcony. Quickly we got a ladder, climbed it and looked inside the room! We saw Grandshaykh ق and Mawlana Shaykh held hands, and Mawlana Shaykh began to tremble. Grandshaykh was not speaking; he was moving his lips and then stopping. Mawlana Shaykh began to tremble more, and also began to move. This lasted for half-an-hour, then they stopped holding hands.

We entered their room and asked Mawlana Shaykh, "What happened?" Because we were so close to him, we were pushing him.

He said, "He was pouring into my heart secrets of the Naqshbandi-Sufi Order that he is delivering to me and *inshāAllāh* I will explain."

Grandshaykh ق ordered Mawlana Shaykh to go to Madīnatu 'l-Munawwarah and for me and my brother to accompany him. He also ordered Mawlana Shaykh to pass those secret knowledges to us, and we wrote what he told us.

In any case, this was and is the way *awlīyāullāh* pour knowledge into hearts. Some pour with their eyes, some pour through the heart, some through holding the hands and arms. This is what we witnessed from Grandshaykh's ق pouring into the heart of Mawlana Shaykh Nazim. We don't know what he poured, but it was for his *khalīfah,* which he did not announce until he gave us the will.

This is a lesson that is not advisable for anyone to say, "I am *khalīfah* of the shaykh;" it is bad manners. How can you address yourself as *khalīfah* when the shaykh is living? You can carry the title out of respect from the shaykh to you, but that sacred knowledge intended for the true *khalīfah* can only be poured into that one's heart.

This is how *awlīyāullāh* pass their secrets from one to another. It's not a simple way. To be a genuine *khalīfah,* you must be mentioned in their will; otherwise, you are not that real one. The shaykh can mention in his will one, two, three, four, ten, as many as he likes; it's up to him. Grandshaykh ق wrote in his will, "I have one *khalīfah,* Nazim Effendi. I did a lot of seclusions for him, and by order of Prophet ﷺ I dressed him with that *khilāfah.* He carried all my secrets, and I gave him two helpers, Hisham and Adnan."

May Allāh ﷻ grant Sayyidi Shaykh Muhammad Nazim Adil al-Haqqani long life! A father is difficult to find; you can easily get a child, but not a father. May Allāh keep that spiritual father to be with us and to give us long life with him, in order to see Sayyīdīna Mahdī ؑ!

With this, we have explained in detail why it is important to know and understand our limits, so that we do not go beyond the bounds of appropriate behavior.

Recently Mawlana Shaykh has been speaking often about what is coming in the future. May Allāh ﷻ bring Sayyīdīna Mahdī ؑ and peace on Earth as soon as possible! *Amīn*.

*As salāmu ʿalaykum wa raḥmatullāhi wa barakātuh.*

*Wa min Allāhi 't-tawfīq, bi ḥurmati 'l-ḥabīb, bi ḥurmati 'l-Fātiḥah.*

*And with Allāh is success. For the sake of the Beloved, for his sake we recite the opening chapter of Holy Qur'an.*

# Islamic Calendar and Holy Days

The Islamic calendar is lunar-based, with twelve months of 29 or 30 days and a year of 354 days. A lunar year is shorter than a solar year, so Muslim holy days cycle back through the Gregorian (Western) calendar. This is how, for example, Ramadan is celebrated at different times of the year, as the annual Islamic calendar is ten days shorter than the Gregorian calendar.

Four months are sacred, in which war is prohibited, unless Muslims are attacked and must defend themselves: Muharram, Rajab, Dhūl-Qʿadah and Dhūl-Hijjah. Holy months include "God's Month" (Rajab), "Prophet's Month" (Shaʿbān) and the "Month of the People" (Ramadan), in which pious acts are deeply rewarded.

## Months of the Islamic Calendar

| | |
|---|---|
| 1. Muḥarram | 7. Rajab |
| 2. Ṣafar | 8. Shaʿbān |
| 3. Rabīʿ ul-Awwal (Rabīʿ I) | 9. Ramaḍān |
| 4. Rabīʿ uth-Thānī (Rabīʿ II) | 10. Shawwāl |
| 5. Jumāda al-Awwal (Jumādi I) | 11. Dhū'l-Qʿadah |
| 6. Jumāda uth-Thāni (Jumādi II) | 12. Dhū'l-Ḥijjah |

## al-Hijrah

The 1st of Muḥarram marks the beginning of the Islamic New Year, chosen because it is the anniversary of Prophet Muhammad's ﷺ historic *Hijrah* (migration) from Mecca to Madinah, where he established the first, preeminent Muslim community in which he introduced unprecedented civil law, human and women's rights, religious tolerance, and military ethics.

## 'Ashūra

On 10th Muḥarram, ʿAshūrā commemorates many sacred events, such as Noah's ark coming to rest, the birth of Abraham, and the building of the Kaʿaba in Mecca. It is also the day on which Sayyīdinā al-Ḥusayn was martyred at Karbala. ʿAshūrā is a major holy day, marked with two days of fasting on the 9th/10th or on 10th/11th based on a holy tradition *(ḥadīth)* of Sayyīdinā Muhammad ﷺ.

## Mawlid

Mawlid an-Nabī, 12th Rabiʿ al-Awwal, commemorates Prophet Muhammad's birth in 570 CE. Mawlid is celebrated globally throughout this month in huge communal gatherings in which a famous poem "Qasīdat al-Burdah" is recited, accompanied by drummers, illustrious poetry recitals and religious singing, eloquent sermons, gift giving, feasts, and feeding the poor. Most Muslim nations observe Mawlid as a national holiday.

## Laylat al-Isra wal-Mi'raj

Literally, "the Night Journey and Ascension;" 27th of Rajab is when Sayyīdīna Muhammad ﷺ physically traveled from Mecca to Jerusalem, ascended through all the levels of Heaven from a rock in the Dome of the Rock, and returned to Mecca—while his bed was still warm. In the Night Journey, Islam's five daily prayers were ordained by God. Sayyīdīna Muhammad also prayed with Abraham, Moses, and Jesus in Jerusalem's al-Aqsa Mosque, signifying that Muslims, Christians, and Jews follow one god. This holy event designated Jerusalem as the third holiest site in Islam, after Mecca and Madinah.

## Laylat al-Bara'ah

"Night of Freedom from Fire" occurs on 15th Shaʿbān. On this night God's Mercy is great; hence, the night is spent reciting

Holy Qur'an and special prayers, as well as visiting the deceased.

## Ramaḍān

Many regard Ramaḍān, the 9th month of the Islamic calendar, the holiest month of the year. Muslims observe a strict fast and participate in pious activities such as charitable giving and peace making. It is a time of intense spiritual renewal for those who observe it. Fasting is meant to instill social awareness of the needy, and to promote gratitude for God's endless favors. The fast is typically broken in a communal setting, and hence Ramadan is a highly social month. At night, a special Ramadan prayer known as "Tarāwīḥ" is offered in congregation, in which one-thirtieth of the Holy Qur'an is recited by the *imām* (prayer leader); thus the entire holy book of 6,000 verses is recited in this month.

## Eid al-Fitr

"Festival of Fast-Breaking" marks the end of Ramadan and is celebrated the first three days of Shawwāl. It is a time for charity and celebration with family and friends for completing a month of blessings and joy. In the Last Days of Ramadan, each Muslim family gives "Zakāt al- Fiṭr" (charity of fast-breaking) which consists of cash and/or food, to help the poor. On the first early morning of Eid, Muslims observe a special congregational prayer, such as Christmas/Easter Mass or the High Holy Days. After Eid prayer is a time to visit family and friends, and give gifts and money (especially to children). Many specialty foods and sweets are prepared solely for Eid days. In most Muslim countries, the entire three days of Eid is a national holiday.

## Yawm al-Arafat

"Day of 'Arafat," the 9th Dhul-Hijjah, occurs just before the celebration of 'Eid al-Aḍḥā. Pilgrims on Hajj assemble for the "standing" on the plain of 'Arafat, located outside Mecca, where they contemplate the Day of Standing (Resurrection Day). Muslims elsewhere in the world fast this day, and gather at a local mosque for prayers. Thus, those who cannot perform Hajj that year still honor the sacrifice of Abraham.

## Eid al-Adha

The "Feast of Sacrifice," celebrated from the $10^{th}$-$13^{th}$ Dhul-Ḥijjah, marks Prophet Abraham's willingness to sacrifice his son Ismāʿīl on God's order. To honor this event, Muslims perform Hajj, the pilgrimage to Mecca that is incumbent on every mature Muslim once in their life if they have the means. Celebrations begin with an animal sacrifice to commemorate Sayyīdīna Ibrāhīm's sacrifice. In Islam, he is known as *Khalīlullāh*, "God's friend." Many consider him the first Muslim and a premiere role model, for his obedience to God and willingness to sacrifice his only child without even questioning the command.

# *Glossary*

*ʿabd* (pl. ʿIbād): lit. slave, servant.
*ʿAbdAllāh*: Lit., "servant of God"
*Abū Bakr aṣ-Ṣiddīq*: the closest Companion of Prophet Muḥammad; the Prophet's father-in-law, who shared the *Hijrah* with him. After the Prophet "s death, he was elected the first caliph (successor); known as one of the most saintly Companions.
*Abū Yazīd/Bayāzīd Bistāmī*: A great ninth century walī and a master of the Naqshbandi Golden Chain.
*adab*: good manners, proper etiquette.
*adhān*: call to prayer.
*Ākhirah:* the Hereafter; afterlife.
*al-*: Arabic definite article, "the"
*ʿalamīn*: world; universes.
*Alḥamdūlillāh*: praise God.
*ʿAlī ibn Abī Ṭālib*: first cousin of Prophet Muhammad, married to his daughter Fāṭimah; fourth caliph.
*alif*: first letter of Arabic alphabet.
*ʿAlīm, al-*: the Knower, a divine attribute
*Allāh*: proper name for God in Arabic.
*Allāhu Akbar*: God is Greater.
*ʿāmal*: good deed (pl. *ʿamāl*).
*amīr* (pl., *umarā*): chief, leader, head of a nation or people.
*anā*: first person singular pronoun
*anbīyā*: prophets (sing. *nabī*).
*ʿaql*: intellect, reason; from the root *ʿaqila*: lit., "to fetter."
*ʿArafah, ʿArafat*: a plain near Mecca where pilgrims gather for the principal rite of Hajj.
*ʿarif*: knower, Gnostic; one who has reached spiritual knowledge of his Lord.
*ʿārifūnʿ bi ʿl-Lāh*: knowers of God.
*Ar-Raḥīm*: The Mercy-Giving, Merciful, Munificent, one of Allāh's ninety-nine Holy Names.
*Ar-Raḥmān*: The Most Merciful, Compassionate, Beneficent; the most repeated of Allāh's Holy Names.
*ʿarsh, al-*: the Divine Throne.
*aṣl*: root, origin, basis.
*astāghfirullah*: lit. "I seek Allāh's forgiveness."
*Awlīyāullāh*: saints of Allāh (sing. *walī*).
*āyah/āyāt* (pl. *Ayāt*): a verse of the Holy Qurʿan.
*Āyat al-Kursī*: "Verse of the Throne," a well-known supplication from the Qurʿan (2:255).

*ʿAzrāʿīl*: the Archangel of Death.
*Badīʿ al-*: The Innovator; a divine name.
*Banī Ādam*: Children of Adam; humanity.
*Bayt al-Maqdis*: the Sacred Mosque in Jerusalem, built at the site where Solomon's Temple was later erected.
*Bayt al-Maʿmūr*: much-frequented house; this refers to the Kaʿbah of the heavens, which is the prototype of the Kaʿbah on Earth, circumambulated by the angels.
*bayaʿ ʿ*: pledge; in the context of this book, the pledge of initiation of a disciple (*murīd*) to a shaykh.
*Bismillāhi'r-Raḥmāni'r-Raḥīm*: "In the name of the All-Merciful, the All-Compassionate"; introductory verse to all chapters of the Qurʿan, except the ninth.
*Dajjāl*: the False Messiah (Anti-Christ) will appear at the end-time of this world, who will deceive Mankind with false divinity.
*dalālah*: evidence.
*dhāt*: self / selfhood.
*dhawq* (pl. *adhwāq*): tasting; technical term referring to the experiential aspect of gnosis.
*dhikr*: remembrance, mention of God through His Holy Names or phrases of glorification.
*ḍīyā*: light.
*Diwān al-Awlīyā*: the nightly gathering of saints with Prophet Muhammad in the spiritual realm.
*duʿa*: supplication.
*dunyā*: world; worldly life.
*ʿEid*: festival; the two major celebrations of Islam are ʿEid al-Fitr, after Ramadan; and ʿEid al-Adha, the Festival of Sacrifice during the time of Hajj, which commemorates the sacrifice of Prophet Abraham.
*farḍ*: obligatory worship.
*Fātiḥah: Sūratu 'l-Fātiḥah*; the opening chapter of the Qurʿan.
*Ghafūr, al-*: The Forgiver; one of the Holy Names of God.
*ghawth*: lit. "Helper"; the highest rank of all saints.
*ghaybuʿ l-muṭlaq, al-*: the absolute unknown; known only to God.
*ghusl*: full shower/bath obligated by a state of ritual impurity, performed before worship.
*Grandshaykh*: generally, a *walī* of great stature. In this text, where spelled "Grandshaykh," refers to Mawlana ʿAbdAllāh ad-Dāghestānī (d. 1973), Mawlana Shaykh Nazim's master.

*hā'*: the Arabic letter ه
*ḥadīth Nabawī* (pl., *āḥadīth*): prophetic *ḥadīth* whose meaning and linguistic expression are those of Prophet Muhammad.
*Ḥadīth Qudsī*: divine saying whose meaning directly reflects the meaning God intended but whose linguistic expression is not divine speech as in the Qur'an.
*ḥaḍr*: present
*Hajj*: the sacred pilgrimage of Islam obligatory on every mature Muslim once in their life.
*ḥalāl*: permitted, lawful according to Islamic Sharī'ah.
*ḥaqīqah, al-*: reality of existence; ultimate truth.
*ḥaqq*: truth
*Ḥaqq, al-*: the Divine Reality, one of the 99 divine names.
*ḥarām*: forbidden, unlawful.
*ḥasanāt:* good deeds.
*hāshā*: God forbid.
*ḥarf*: (pl. *ḥurūf*) letter; Arabic root "edge."
*Ḥawā*: Eve.
*ḥaywān*: animal.
*Hijrah*: emigration.
*ḥikmah*: wisdom.
*ḥujjah*: proof.
*hūwa*: the pronoun "he," made up of the Arabic letters *hā'* and *wāw* .
*'ibādu 'l-Lāh*: servants of God.
*'ifrīt*: a type of Jinn, huge and powerful.
*iḥsān*: doing good, "It is to worship God as though you see Him; for if you are not seeing Him, He sees you."
*ikhlāṣ, al-:* sincere devotion.
*ilāh:* (pl. *āliha*): idols or gods.
*ilāhīyya*: divinity.
*ilhām*: divine inspiration sent to *awlīyāullāh*.
*'ilm*: knowledge, science.
*'ilmu 'l-awrāq*: knowledge of papers.
*'ilmu 'l-adhwāq*: knowledge of taste.
*'ilmu 'l-ḥurūf*: science of letters.
*'ilmu 'l-kalām*: scholastic theology.
*'ilmun ladunnī*: divinely inspired knowledge.
*imān*: faith, belief.
*imām*: leader of congregational prayer; an advanced scholar followed by a large community.
*insān*: humanity; pupil of the eye.
*insānu 'l-kāmil, al-*: the Perfect Man, *i.e.*, Prophet Muhammad.
*irādatullāh*: the Will of God.
*irshād*: spiritual guidance.
*ism*: name.
*isma-Llāh*: name of God.
*isrā'*: night journey; used here in reference to the night

journey of Prophet Muhammad.
*Isrāʿfīl*: Archangel Rafael, in charge of blowing the Final Trumpet.
*jalāl*: majesty.
*jamāl*: beauty.
*jamaʿa*: group, congregation.
*Jannah*: Paradise.
*jihād*: to struggle in God's Path.
*Jibrīl*: Archangel Gabriel of revelation.
*Jinn*: a species of living beings created from fire, invisible to most humans. Jinn can be Muslims or non-Muslims.
*Jumuʿah*: Friday congregational prayer, held in a large mosque.
*Kaʿbah*: the first House of God, located in Mecca, Saudi Arabia to which pilgrimage is made and to which Muslims face in prayer.
*kāfir*: unbeliever.
*Kalāmullāh al-Qadīm*: lit., Allāh's Ancient Words, *viz.* the Holy Qurʿan.
*kalīmat at-tawḥīd: lā ilāha illa-Llāh:* "There is no god but Al-Lah (the God)."
*karāmat:* miracles.
*khalīfah*: deputy.
*Khāliq, al-*: the Creator, one of 99 divine names.
*khalq*: Creation.
*khāniqah*: designated smaller place for worship other than a mosque; *zāwiyahh.*
*khuluq*: conduct, manners.
*Kirāmun Kātabīn*: Honored Scribe angels.
*lā*: no; not; not existent; the particle of negation.
*lā ilāha illa-Llāh Muḥammadun Rasūlullāh*: there is no deity except Allāh, Muhammad is the Messenger of Allāh.
*lām*: Arabic letter ل.
*al-Lawḥ* al-*Maḥfūẓ*: the Preserved Tablets.
*Laylat al-Isrāʿ wa'l-Miʿrāj*: the Night Journey and Ascension of Prophet Muhammad to Jerusalem and to the seven heavens.
*Madīnātu 'l-Munawwarah*: the Illuminated city; city of Prophet Muhammad; Madinah.
*mahr*: dowry, given by the groom to the bride.
*Malakūt:* divine kingdom.
*Malik, al-*: the Sovereign, a divine name.
*Mālik*: Archangel of Hell.
*maqām*: spiritual station; tomb of a prophet, messenger or saint.
*maʿrifah*: gnosis.
*māshāllah*: as Allāh Wills.
*Mawlānā*: lit. "our master" or "our patron," referring to an esteemed person.
*maẓhar*: place of disclosure.
*miḥrāb*: prayer niche.
*Mikāīl*: Archangel of rain.

*mīzān*: the scale that weighs our deeds on Judgment Day.
*mīm*: Arabic letter م.
*minbar*: pulpit.
*Miracles*: of *awlīyā*, known as *karamāt*; of prophets, known as *muʿjizāt* (lit., "That which renders powerless or helpless").
*miʿrāj*: the ascension of Prophet. Muhammad from Jerusalem to the seven heavens.
*Muḥammadun rasūlu 'l-Lāh:* Muhammad is the Messenger of God.
*mulk, al-*: the World of dominion.
*Muʿmin, al-*: Guardian of Faith, one of the 99 Names of God.
*muʿmin*: a believer.
*munājāt*: invocation to God in a very intimate form.
*Munkir*: one of the angels of the grave.
*murīd*: disciple, student, follower.
*murshid*: spiritual guide; *pir*.
*mushāhadah*: direct witnessing.
*mushrik* (pl. *mushrikūn*): idolater; polytheist.
*muwwaḥid* (pl. *muwaḥḥidūn*): those who affirm God's Oneness.
*nabī*: a prophet of God.
*nāfs:* lower self, ego.
*Nakīr*: the other angel of the grave (with Munkir).
*nūr*: light.
*Nūḥ*: the prophet Noah.
*Nūr, an-*: "The Source of Light"; a divine name.
*Qādir, al-*: "The Powerful"; a divine name.
*qalam, al-*: the Pen.
*qiblah*: direction, specifically, the direction faced by Muslims during prayer and other worship, towards the Sacred House in Mecca.
*Quddūs, al-*: "The Holy One"; a divine name.
*qurb*: nearness
*quṭb* (pl. *aqṭāb*): axis or pole. Among the poles are:
*Quṭbu 'l-bilād*: Pole of the Lands.
*Quṭbu 'l-irshād*: Pole of Guidance.
*Quṭbu 'l-aqṭāb*: Pole of Poles.
*Quṭbu 'l-ʿaẓam*: Greatest Pole.
*Quṭbu 'l-mutaṣarrif*: Pole of Affairs.
*al-quṭbīyyatu 'l-kubrā*: the highest station of poleship.
*Rabb, ar-*: the Lord.
*Raḥīm, ar-*: "The Most Compassionate"; a divine name.
*Raḥmān, ar-:* "The All-Merciful"; a divine name.
*raḥmāh*: mercy.
*rakaʿat*: one full set of prescribed motions in prayer. Each prayer consists of a one or more *rakaʿats*.
*Ramadān*: the ninth month of the Islamic calendar; month of fasting.

*Rasūl*: a messenger of God.
*Rasūlullāh*: the Messenger of God, Muhammad ﷺ.
*Rāūf, ar-*: "The Most Kind"; a divine name.
*Razzāq, ar-*: "The Provider"; a divine name.
*rawḥānīyyah*: spirituality; spiritual essence of something.
*Riḍwān*: Archangel of Paradise.
*rizq*: provision; sustenance.
*rūḥ*: spirit. *Ar-Rūḥ* is the name of a great angel.
*rukūʿ*: bowing posture of the prayer.
*ṣadaqah*: voluntary charity.
*ṣaḥīḥ*: authentic; term certifying validity of a *ḥadīth* of the Prophet.
*ṣāim*: fasting person (pl. *ṣāimūn*)
*salām*: peace.
*Salām, as-*: "The Peaceful"; a divine name.
*as-salāmu ʿalaykum*: "Peace be upon you" (Islamic greeting).
*ṣalāt*: Islam's ritual prayer.
*Ṣalāt an-Najāt*: prayer of salvation, offered in the late hours of night.
*Ṣamad, aṣ-*: Self-Sufficient, upon whom creatures depend.
*Ṣaḥābah* (sing., sahabi): Companions of the Prophet; the first Muslims.
*sajda* (pl. *sujūd*): prostration.
*ṣalāt*: prayer, one of the five obligatory pillars of Islam. Also, to invoke blessing on the Prophet.
*ṣalawāt* (sing. *ṣalāt*): invoking blessings and peace upon the Prophet.
*ṣawm, ṣiyām*: fasting.
*sayyīāt*: bad deeds.
*sayyid*: leader; also, a descendant of Prophet Muhammad.
Sayyīdīnā: our master (fem. *sayyidunā; sayyidatunā*: our mistress).
*shahādah*: lit. testimony; the testimony of Islamic faith: *Lā ilāha illa 'l-Lāh wa Muḥammadun rasūlu 'l-Lāh*, "There is no god but Allāh, the One God, and Muhammad is the Messenger of God."
*Shah Naqshband*: Grandshaykh Muhammad Bahauddin Shah-Naqshband, a great eighth century walī, the founder of the Naqshbandi Ṭarīqah.
*shaykh*: lit. "old man," a religious guide, teacher; master of spiritual discipline.
*shifāʾ*: cure.
*shirk*: polytheism, idolatry, ascribing partners to God
*ṣiffāt*: attributes; term referring to Divine Attributes.
*Silsilat adh-dhahabīyya*: "Golden Chain" of spiritual authority in Islam

*sohbet* (Arabic, *ṣuḥbah*): association: the assembly or discourse of a shaykh.
*subḥanAllāh*: glory be to God.
*sulṭān/sulṭānah*: ruler, monarch.
Sulṭān al-Awlīyā: lit., "King of the *awlīyā*; the highest-ranking saint.
*Sūnnah*: Practices of Prophet Muhammad in actions and words; what he did, said, recommended, or approved of in his Companions.
*sūrah*: a chapter of the Qur'an; picture, image.
*Sūratu 'l- Ikhlāṣ*: Chapter 114 of Holy Qur'an; the Chapter of Sincerity.
*ṭabīb*: doctor.
*tābi'īn*: the Successors, one generation after the Prophet's Companions.
*tafsīr*: to explain, expound, explicate, or interpret; technical term for commentary or exegesis of the Holy Qur'ān.
*tajallī* (pl. *tajallīyāt*): theophanies, God's self-disclosures, Divine Self-manifestation.
*takbīr*: lit. "Allāhu Akbar," God is Great.
*tarawīḥ*: the special nightly prayers of Ramadan.
*ṭarīqat/ṭarīqah*: lit., way, road or path. An Islamic order or path of discipline and devotion under a guide or shaykh; Sufism.
*tasbīḥ*: recitation glorifying or praising God.
*tawāḍa'*: humbleness.
*ṭawāf*: the rite of circumambulating the Ka'bah while glorifying God during Hajj and 'Umrah.
*tawḥīd*: unity; universal or primordial Islam, submission to God, as the sole Master of destiny and ultimate Reality.
*Tawrāt*: Torah
*tayammum*: Alternate ritual ablution performed in the absence of water.
*'ubūdīyyah*: state of worshipfulness. Servanthood
*'ulamā* (sing. *'alim* ): scholars.
*'ulūmu 'l-awwalīna wa 'l-ākhirīn*: knowledge of the "Firsts" and the "Lasts" refers to the knowledge God poured into the heart of Prophet Muhammad during his ascension to the Divine Presence.
*'ulūm al-Islāmī*: Islamic religious sciences.
*Ummah*: faith community, nation.
*'Umar ibn al-Khaṭṭāb*: an eminent Companion of Prophet Muhammad and second caliph of Islam.
'Umrah: the minor pilgrimage to Mecca, performed at any time of the year.

*'Uthmān ibn 'Affān*: eminent Companion of the Prophet; his son-in-law and third caliph of Islam, renowned for compiling the Qur'an.
*walad*: a child.
*waladī*: my child.
*walāyah*: proximity or closeness; sainthood.
*walī* (pl. *awlīyā*): saint, or "he who assists"; guardian; protector.
*wasīlah*: a means; holy station of Prophet Muhammad as God's intermediary to grant supplications.
*wāw*: Arabic letter و
*wujūd, al-*: existence; "to find," "the act of finding," as well as "being found."
*Y'aqūb*: Jacob; the prophet.
*yamīn*: the right hand; previously meant "oath."
*Yawm al-'ahdi wa'l-mīthāq:* Day of Oath and Covenant, a heavenly event before this Life, when all souls of humanity were present to God, and He took from each the promise to accept His Sovereignty as Lord.
*Yawm al-Qiyāmah:* Day of Judgment.
*Yūsuf*: Joseph; the prophet.
*zāwiyah*: designated smaller place for worship other than a mosque; also *khāniqah*.
*zīyārah*: visitation to the grave of a prophet, a prophet's companion or a saint.

# Other Publications of Interest

## Mawlana Shaykh Nazim Adil al-Haqqani

- The Sufilive Series (2010)
- Through the Eye of the Needle
- The Healing Power of Sufi Meditation
- The Path to Spiritual Excellence
- In the Mystic Footsteps of Saints, 2 volumes
- Liberating the Soul, 6 volumes

## Mawlana Shaykh Hisham Kabbani

- The Sufilive Series (2010)
- Cyprus Summer Series, 2 vols
- The Nine-fold Ascent
- Who Are the Guides?
- Illuminations
- Banquet for the Soul
- Symphony of Remembrance
- Healing Power of Sufi Meditation
- In the Shadow of Saints
- Keys to the Divine Kingdom
- The Sufi Science of Self-Realization
- Universe Rising
- Approach of Armageddon?
- Pearls and Coral, 2 vols
- Classical Islam and the Naqshbandi Sufi Tradition
- Naqshbandi Sufi Way
- Encyclopedia of Islamic Doctrine, 7 volumes
- Angels Unveiled
- Encyclopedia of Muhammad's Women Companions and the Traditions They Related

## Hajjah Amina Adil

- Muhammad: the Messenger of Islam
- The Light of Muhammad
- Lore of Light / Links of Light
- My Little Lore of Light, 3 volumes

## Hajjah Naziha Adil Kabbani

- Secrets of Heavenly Food (2009)
- Heavenly Foods (2001)

www.ingramcontent.com/pod-product-compliance
Lightning Source LLC
Chambersburg PA
CBHW030321080526
44584CB00012B/661
* 9 7 8 1 9 3 0 4 0 9 7 3 6 *